WHO'S GOT YOUR FINANCIAL BACK?

"We don't stop playing because we grow old;
We grow old because we stop playing."

— *George Bernard Shaw*

WHO'S
GOT
YOUR

Conquering All Challenges
with the Right Advisor

PAUL S. REBACK • CFP®

President of Capital Estate Advisors, Inc.
A Registered Investment Advisory Firm

Who's Got Your Financial Back?
Conquering All Challenges with the Right Advisor

Published by New Voices Press
315 West 70th Street, Suite 6C
New York, NY 10023
212-580-8833

Library of Congress Cataloguing-in-Publication Data

Paul S. Reback, CFP®

Who's Got Your Financial Back?
Conquering All Challenges with the Right Advisor

Published by New Voices Press
ISBN 978-0-9883591-1-6

1. Personal Finance 2. Wealth Management 3. Business & Investing
4. Budgeting & Money Management 5. Retirement Planning

Edited by Judy Katz, Katz Creative, Inc. and Ghostbooksters.com
Cover and Book design by Tony Iatridis, nycartdirector.com
Additional creative input by Amy Pisanelli
Administrative support by Tiani Mattus and Layla Baez
Proofreading and editorial assistance by Maris Finn
Cover photo by Jan Goldstoff
Printing by createspace.com

Dedication

To Al and Leah, my incredible parents.
Thank you for the gift of unconditional love, the gift of humor,
and the gift of self-esteem.

Acknowledgements

First, I want to give a shout-out to my editor, Judy Katz. In the two years it has taken us to complete this book, her creativity and enthusiasm never diminished. When, in the course of our work, Judy decided to turn her portfolio over to me to manage, I knew that she truly got the ironclad commitment I make to every one of my clients. I could not have had a better partner in this project.

My life has been filled with an abundance of blessings: the greatest blessings have always been the people in my life--and one small dog.

MY HEARTFELT THANKS GO TO:

Catherine and Lorraine: for your unconditional love and support.

Tom: for your lifelong confidence, guidance, wisdom and humor.

Amy: for being the most amazing ally and sounding-board one could ever have. You are defined by words such as warrior, loyalty, competence and now--new mom!

Tiani: for your exactitude and discipline in keeping us on the right path, always.

Dave: for your sharing, your excellence, and your generous gifts of time and perspective.

My Counselors and Associates Bernie and Mike,
John O and Flaxman for your remarkable direction
and always timely and generous assistance.

Jeffrey Gunthorpe ("Jeff Guns"):
for getting me in the best shape of my life.

My Amazing friends, Johnny, JJ, Scott, Tom
(yes Tom you get two shout-outs): for so many great times
and laughter, even in (especially in) the tough times.

PAUL'S POWER: Paul, Paul and Paul, comprising the
greatest Rock Band in the World!

All of our clients: thank you for your trust, and for
the many life lessons you taught me.

And last but not least, to Teddy. For all you gave, you were
the greatest dog on the planet, and you will be deeply missed--
even as you wag your tail in heaven and make the angels smile.
Anyone who loves a canine will understand. RIP, my friend.

"I will tell you how to become rich:
Close the doors.
Be fearful when others are greedy.
Be greedy when others are fearful."

— *Warren Buffett*

Table of Contents

"The best time to plant a tree was 20 years ago. The second best time is now."

— *Chinese Proverb*

Preface

Why You Need an Outsider's POV
When It Comes to Your Money

Money is the least of your problems. You may not believe me. You picked up this book to learn how to put some aside so you can build what you have into more, learn how to spend it wisely, and how to use it. Well, I am going to tell you how to achieve all of that – and more. If you follow my advice, you will be a lot more secure. However, for this journey we are about to embark on together, I am going to show you not only how to have the degree of wealth you want and need, but also how to have a richer life.

As a financial advisor and wealth manager, I work with people from all walks of life, from multi-millionaires with complicated lives to hard-working middle class individuals and couples with modest nest eggs and equally complicated lives. After all, whose life is not complicated?

My goal is to encourage, challenge, educate, and inspire you, the reader, to take a more active role in your financial future. In the following chapters, I tell stories about how a little planning and a lot of trust can go a very long way. Some stories deal with my own personal and familial matters, and others center on clients and friends. Some of these stories are inspiring, and some are cautionary, but I am certain that all of them will be useful to you in moving forward with your financial plans.

They say hindsight is 20/20, which is why I open the book with my own family's financial history. Had my parents had the foresight to make definite plans in terms of retirement funds and life insurance – before my father got sick and before my mother was left to struggle with the family business, for which she was greatly unprepared – perhaps my mother would have been able to live out her remaining years in peace, rather than hardship. I begin this way, not to ask for your sympathy, but so that you can learn from my family's missteps and have the foresight to start your planning now.

As in life, families are a huge part of this book. They can range from being a tried-and-true support system, to being a brute, antagonistic force. One of my clients, whose story is explored in detail in the book, has four financially dependent adult children who cause their father many headaches. In fact, many of my clients have financially dependent adult children. I offer their stories to show that while there is nothing wrong with having dependents and involving your family in your finances, they must not be allowed to be draining, either in the arena of money or morale.

You might be saying, "Why do I need this book? I know how much money I have and what I want to do with it." Perhaps you're right, and you do know exactly how to invest your money yourself, but you are in the minority. I think it's important for people from all walks of life to have a financial manager working for you, whether you think you can handle it yourself or not. We allow you to keep living your life, working at your job and raising your families, without having to micromanage your assets. Leave that task up to us. I will be the first to admit that being a financial manager is not easy. It takes patience, moxie, and heart, as well as a finely tuned ear to the financial climate –excellent math skills don't hurt either!

I've been working as a Financial Advisor for many years, and I can tell you that being entrusted with other people's money is no small potatoes. You have someone's – or more often an entire family's – life in your hands. I like to imagine that I'm dealing with my own money each time, because that is how important my clients are to me. I believe this is where so many other advisors fail. They tend to put their own needs ahead of their clients', and don't take into account the consequences attached to someone else's fortune. It is no wonder that once the Madoff scandal broke, people started getting even more careful about who to trust with their money – for good reason! Celebrities, professional athletes, and too many average Joes have fallen victim to shoddy investors.

While some financial advisors may seem to have you and your money's best interests in mind, if they don't possess the tenacity, the experience, and the passion for caring about you and your family as their own, your estate might be in danger. That is why I've written this book – I care about your money as much as and maybe more than you do. You need to find that kind of person for your financial future.

Defining Wealth

How do you define wealth? I will devote a lot of time to this question, and provide examples of people who define wealth in vastly different ways than you might expect. This may sound like a cheeky thing to say, especially coming from someone who works in finance, but I truly believe that wealth is something each person must define on his or her own terms. Wealth transcends the physical green paper and how much of it you accumulate: what's more important is how you incorporate it into your life. Do you control your money, or does your money control you?

One client that I have been working with for a long time is an older man who has become as close to me as my own family. He has a fortune that can rival some of the top-earning celebrities in Hollywood, but that doesn't stop him from penny-pinching. He is laser-focused on his funds and is steadfast about staying on top of them. While some financial managers might become frustrated with a man like him and write him off as a "miser" or a "cheapskate," he has actually become one of my most beloved clients. In addition to my doing it for them, some people feel the need to keep track of the seemingly minor details, for it is in those tiny details that massive mistakes can be made if you aren't meticulous.

So why do people seek out financial managers? Is it just to have them count pebbles and balance books? Not at all. Some of the major reasons people seek me out, for example, include: planning for retirement, expanding their properties and learning how to invest (buying a second home or building a vacation compound for their family), how to invest an inheritance, building a balanced portfolio, or creating a nest egg to leave to their children. I have had clients who want to do all the aforementioned, or have other plans in mind.

I will tell you that my views on retirement are not for the faint-of-heart – as I see it, most older people these days are still living vibrant, exciting lives. My ideas may veer from the traditional and seem more radical than you're used to, but if you give me a chance, you will see that I truly do have your best interests in mind.

Ultimately, the relationship between a client and a financial advisor is a special one, and you shouldn't be frustrated if it doesn't come easy at first. You will have to feel each other out and make sure there is mutual trust, and that your personalities are compatible. I have clients with whom I talk almost every day, and others I speak with once every few months. No matter what, we have to be able to respect and trust each other. The process of finding an ideal financial manager is part alchemy, part courtship. I believe that this book is the first step in showing you how to capture that magic. The idea is for you to be completely comfortable, knowing your assets are in good hands now, and that they will continue to serve all your needs and desires, well into the future.

"In three words I can sum up everything I've learned about life: it goes on."

— *Robert Frost*

1

Surprises: Learning How to Take the Unexpected in Stride

Before I dive into the nitty-gritty of financial planning, which is presumably the main reason you picked up this book, I want to begin by sharing some of my personal history with you. I've found that looking back is useful. I don't mean that I lament what could have been, but rather than mining my family's past – at times a frustrating experience – it helps provide a roadmap to a better future for myself, and is something I encourage my clients to do too. By explaining where I came from, I hope you will gain valuable insight into why I am so passionate about my career and helping people like you.

Like many people, I wasn't able to fully appreciate my parents until I was an adult. As children we have a tendency to view our parents as looming, idyllic figures. It wasn't until I became a parent myself that I realized just how hard my parents worked, and how they could have worked smarter to be better prepared when hard times knocked at our door.

A Not-So Simple Bronx Tale

I was born in the Bronx, about a block away from Yankee Stadium. When I was a kid, I could always tell when the New York Yankees were playing. From my window I could see the Yankees' flags flying proudly around Yankee Stadium. When summer ended, taking baseball with it, football reigned supreme, and the New York Giants replaced the Yankees on game day. The crowds

7

packed into the stadium were so loud that the roar would seep through my windows. It quickly became the soundtrack to my childhood. Watching baseball games on TV now doesn't even come close, but every time I hear a crowd swell with cheers for a home run, it takes me back to those summer afternoons. It really was a phenomenal area in which to grow up.

The stadium had several fields in the surrounding neighborhood where both semi-professional and little league teams played when the Yankees weren't playing. I played there with my friends, too. On the days I wasn't playing with my friends, my dad and I would go down and watch these games together. He would always wear his white tank top and his moccasins with socks – it was quite a look. After watching an inning or two, he'd pull two dollars from his pocket and say, "Go get us a hot dog." There would be a truck parked outside and I'd get two hot dogs with sauerkraut and mustard, and two Sun Dews to wash it all down. I'll always cherish those weekends. They weren't much, but they were some of the only one-on-one moments I had with him – he was constantly working, and I rarely saw him during the weekdays.

A Father's Struggle

My father was a distributor specializing in miniature lighting. If you've ever seen the inside of an airplane cockpit, all of those dials and lights attached to the dashboard are what he sold. He even started his own business in 1959 on Harrison Street in the Tribeca neighborhood of New York City. It was called Reback Electronics Company. He rented a space in the building that housed the Commodities Exchange, which was essentially one large room. As a kid, I would go down there and have no idea why all these men in white shirts and ties were in this building, where my father of modest means was toiling away in his business.

My father never went to college, and only went to high school for one year. I still don't know exactly how he got into that business. Prior to that, he worked at Lafayette Radio and didn't like his lifestyle, so he quit and started Reback Electronics. Unfortunately, health was never my father's strong suit. He suffered a minor stroke a few years before I was born, and then, when I was five years old, had a major heart attack. I remember the day that it happened vividly. I was with him. I was never able to play ball and wrestle with him like other children did with their fathers, which is why most of our weekends were spent watching sports rather than playing them. I always felt like I was missing out on something great, like there was a secret bond between father and son that I wasn't allowed in on.

My father's heart attack kept him in the hospital for seven weeks. The treatment today is certainly far superior to what it was back then, but, given that extensive length of time, my mother had to go to work in his business to keep the doors open. The only other employee they had was an elderly man (who I always thought was 90 years old, but now I realize he couldn't have been nearly that old) whose main job was to run deliveries and drop things off at the post office, but also to count the inventory for the shipments. My father always got angry with him because he was convinced he wasn't counting correctly. My mother barely knew what she was doing, but they weren't about to leave the operations to Methuselah. She worked her hardest to keep it running for as long as she could. When my father finally got released from the hospital and went back to work, he became the seller and the advisor, while my mother took the reins of the back office.

Since both of my parents were at the office for long hours, I became a latchkey kid. The relatives on my mother's side lived too far for me to stay with them after school, and even as a young boy I could sense that there was a disparity in our wealth. I never realized it at the time but my parents had no money. Most kids were able to go home for lunch every day because they lived within walking distance and their mothers were home to feed them. My mother worked, so she would pack me a lunch, and I'd have to eat it in the lunchroom. I so badly wanted to be one of those children who were able to spend their lunchtime with their mother, in a warm, comfortable home. I was embarrassed; I did not want to be one of the vast minority of kids who ate my lunch in the school lunchroom, commanded by the intimidating lunch lady, so I started throwing away my lunch. I was hungry, but I hungered for something more than food – respect and a better life for my family.

Every Friday as a treat, I got a dollar. This was when I learned how to stretch a dollar to its fullest capacity. During lunch on Fridays, I'd set out for the store down the street that served food too. A hamburger was forty cents, French fries were twenty cents, and the large chocolate egg cream was fifteen cents. The remaining change would go towards a tip – I always left a tip – and a piece of dime candy. Can you imagine getting an entire meal like that for under a dollar today? It boggles the mind!

A Strong and Fearless Woman

My father died when I was 15. I always knew that his death at a relatively early age was inevitable and that someday my mother and I would be left on our own. Throughout my young life I had prayed to God every night not to take my father away, and for a while my prayers were answered. When it finally happened, the reality of his death was still a shock. His death had a profound effect on me, but my mother took it much harder. Her body nearly crumbled from grief, as though by shrinking herself the news of his death might miss her completely. She lost every hair on her head and had to wear a wig, all the while suffering from asthma, broken toes, gallstones, and so many other physical maladies. Not to mention another burden – I was a somewhat difficult teenager. For example, she didn't want me to go to the Woodstock Festival in 1969, but I wouldn't let up until she agreed, reminding her that before my father died, they had agreed to let me go. Now as a father, I can understand the extra grief this must have caused her.

She never wore this on her sleeve or let it affect her demeanor, though. In fact, many people took to calling her "The Chief" because she was strong and could take charge at a moment's notice. All of my friends would go to talk to her about their problems, and she always had a solution for everybody. She was 4'11 and 110 pounds; she came to this country without knowing a word of English, only speaking Hebrew, Yiddish and Russian. But she became the mom that did it all. She helped me with my homework and made dinner every night

When we were out in public, she was smart, funny and charming, and eventually began volunteering at a hospital. I suppose she needed to keep busy. After my father died, there was no way she was able to keep the business up and running, so she sold it. She only got about 60 grand for it – a forced sale price, but she needed to sell and took the first offer. The money wasn't nearly enough to retire on, but, again, she had no choice. She was no longer in any condition to run a business, and I was still way too young to help her out in any significant way.

Family – Friend, or Foe?

The real kicker here is that I had two uncles who were money savvy. One of them was my mother's brother, Uncle George. He had enough academic credentials to wallpaper the Sistine Chapel: Trinity College undergraduate, Columbia University MBA, New York University Law School, a Fellow in the Society of Actuaries, and the president of a life insurance company. He actually lent my dad some money to help him start the Reback Electronics Company. Another uncle, my Uncle Nat, was a life insurance salesman for another company. Ironically, with all of this education and life experience, neither of them took the time to explain prudent financial planning or decision-making to my parents. In retrospect, a relatively simple conversation warning them about not having sufficient life insurance could have changed many lives, including mine. They knew full well that my father was in ill health, had a dependent wife with a young child, and was running a one-man business that had no assets except for its simple brick and mortar. One conversation with advice that they had undoubtedly given to countless others somehow never came up – something I still wonder about to this day. If these uncles had offered their two cents, or if my parents had any sort of financial guidance from any resource early on, they could have wound up in a much different situation. If only they had established a solid life insurance plan, it would have changed my life and my mother's – giving her peace of mind and greater health instead of dying a broken woman from stress and heartache.

While we seldom saw my father's family, we always had a good time when we all got together…which makes it even more puzzling that after my father's death, they completely fell out of touch. We didn't hear anything from them for nearly 25 years. They wrote us off in a time when we needed family – and good business sense – the most.

Of course, hindsight is – and always will be – 20/20. If we allow ourselves, we can spend our entire lives obsessing over what could have been – it's too easy to slip into that kind of mindset. I was, and still am, frustrated that my parents wound up in those unfortunate circumstances, but I make a conscious effort to be a forward-thinker. Nonetheless, as I said before, it is crucial to learn from past mistakes. The best use of these insights is to help us make better decisions moving forward. The one good thing that did come out of this whole mess was that I am now able to understand my family's missteps and take the necessary measures to ensure that my clients' finances, and my own, will not suffer the same consequences.

What's Your Story?

Perhaps my story will prompt you to delve into your own financial history and discover where you and your family started out. Even the canonized American "rags to riches" story is often glossed over; there are typically twists and turns in all of our personal histories that have been omitted, glamorized or otherwise altered over the years. I find that it can be especially informative and therapeutic to ask questions of your older relatives. You might be surprised by their family stories and wisdom that have been amassed throughout the years.

The financial climate today is much different than it was in the past. While accumulating assets, saving for the future and also being able to pay for your current lifestyle is not a novel concept, what is most needed now, I believe, is a better understanding of how to go about using your assets to create the life you want. To do this intelligently, in the face of a number of unique challenges, you need an expert to help guide you through.

If you have an uncle in the business willing and able to help, consider yourself most fortunate. For everyone else, let me tell you a bit more about the forces that shaped my journey and how these experiences allow me to understand what you want and need in a financial advisor.

"The flower that blooms in adversity is the rarest and most beautiful of all."

— *Mulan, Walt Disney Company*

2

Indirect: The Circuitous Route to my True Calling

A Rock Star Wanna-Be Turned Investment Advisor

When I was born, my father was 45 and my mother was 43 – both a bit old to begin parenting. When my father became ill, he had limited working hours and a strict 9:30 p.m. bedtime. This created a lot of one-on-one time for my mother and me. She talked to me as if I were an adult as far back as I can remember. My opinions were always solicited and validated. It was like I was a Jewish Consigliere, and I loved it.

In retrospect, this was probably too much for a young boy to handle since I was an only child. Nonetheless, this kind of attention and respect for my opinion, not only from my mother but also from several other relatives, had a silver lining. I am convinced that my father's premature death, our lack of financial solvency, and especially my role as my mother's confidante became the impetus for me to become an investment advisor. Talking numbers and finance may make many people's eyes glaze over, but having witnessed the dire consequences brought on by unpreparedness, fiscal responsibility sounds like music to my ears. I also have a special feeling for my elders, and I can honestly say that my ability to earn and keep their trust is one of my greatest sources of pride.

Before I embarked on my career path, however, I have to admit that I was an indifferent college student hoping to break into the music industry—not unlike a lot of future baby boomers, or at least several of the young men of my generation I hung out with. I started college at age 16, which also might have contributed to my lack of motivation. I was a lot more excited about playing shows with my band, in which I was the drummer, than about my classes. I had begun playing the drums at age 13, after being chained to the piano for several years, under great duress. Drums were the way to go: you got lots of attention, especially from the girls in the audience. Besides, my father's nephew Rick played the drums and I thought he was the coolest guy I knew.

At that time, schoolwork could not hold my interest, no matter how hard I tried to focus. I remember sitting in my Geology class thinking, "Why do I have to learn about rocks if I'm going to be a musician?" Instead, I thought about my outfit for the next gig: velvet pants, leather jackets, custom-made black boots with silver stars and 3-inch wooden heels. Now that was something that held my interest! Misguided teen angst aside, it was truly difficult for me to find my place in college. I wound up dropping out and struggling to work in the music industry. Unsurprisingly, during those lean years many of the projects my band and I started eventually met their demise. My bank account was quickly dwindling, our great rehearsal loft in lower Manhattan was burglarized, and our lead singer quit. Everything that happened seemed like a loud-and-clear sign to quit music, but it was all I knew at that point. If not music, then what?

One day, as I was flipping through the Village Voice magazine, half-heartedly looking for a lead singer. I found an ad for a sales job. It read: "HELP WANTED. Sales Representative. Metropolitan Life. $200 a week." I thought of my Uncle George, president of a life insurance company, living on Madison Avenue. It seemed like he was living a pretty good life, so I considered the possibility. Sales sounded like the exact opposite of rock n' roll, but I needed the money. I had reason to question my present and my future. I pushed myself to make the call, and was surprised and pleased to secure an interview for the very next day.

I dusted off my one suit, combed my hair, and walked into the Met Life office. Once pleasantries were over, they said, "You're hired." Wow, I thought. That was fast! Before I could exalt in my good luck, the recruiter continued, "Here's your first assignment, Mr. Reback. It's called Project 100. You will write down the names of 100 people you know, their ages, addresses, relationships, etc." Wait – this was going to be my clientele? I thought to myself. Are these guys out of their minds? No one I know is going to want life insurance.

Of course I did what I was told, and even though there wound up being no potential clients in the meager list I pieced together, they hired me anyway and began paying me $200 a week to learn the ins and outs of the life insurance industry. They started by giving me a huge stack of books to read that contained some pretty in-depth information, and I had flashbacks to those dull lectures and heavy textbooks from college. To my surprise, though, when I cracked the books open I wasn't turned off, alienated, or disinterested. Instead, I sucked up the material like a cactus in the desert. Also, unlike the situation with my former dysfunctional band, selling insurance was the first time I felt like I could excel at something based upon my own ability, without having to depend on other people to make it happen. I could do this on my own and maybe revitalize some of the potential I had let whither in my futile pursuit of rock star fame and fortune.

Once I had worked my way through all those books, I became excited about insurance. Ironically, just as I was beginning to settle into my new career, I got a phone call from the people who represent Johnny Winter, the legendary blues guitarist and pro-

17

ducer. I had always fantasized that someday I would get to play with someone of Johnny Winter's caliber, whether Winter, the Rolling Stones, Cream, or Jimi Hendrix. I never actually thought the opportunity might fall directly into my lap.

Johnny Winter's representative said they had seen me drum with my band and asked me to come in and play a few songs with Johnny! Apparently Johnny was interested in putting a new group together, and they wanted me to be the drummer! I was floored. My face lost all its color and my mind went blank. All I could think about was drumming under hot neon lights, Johnny's long white hair flowing in front of me, and thousands of screaming fans. This was the moment I'd been waiting for all these years, but it couldn't have come at a worse time.

Part of me wanted to say, "Yes, of course!" but I knew I couldn't. For so long I had been preoccupied with trying to become this rock star image I had in my head, but I knew in my heart it wasn't right for me anymore. I was on my way to establishing a legitimate career for myself, and there was no way I was going to sacrifice that for a shot at my 15 minutes of fame. Call it crazy. In retrospect, I call it maturity.

I took a deep breath and told Johnny's representatives, "I appreciate the offer, probably more than you know, but I'm not available." It was a truly life-changing experience for me to turn it down, and I sometimes still think about what would have happened if I'd said yes and took the opportunity. Ultimately, I'm very proud of the career and life I've made for my family and myself, and would not trade it for even the brightest of spotlights. Sadly Johnny died alone in a hotel room while on tour in Europe. I never looked back and regretted my career decision, but when I heard of his death I had a moment of sadness for a man that I revered and would have loved to know better. He was incredible and his music was and is part of the fabric that defines me. RIP Johnny.

Answering the Call, and Making a Few of My Own

I officially began working at MetLife in December 1973. After six months the district manager came to me and said, "We would like you to consider a promotion to sales manager. Instead of building clientele for yourself, you will recruit and train other people to build a clientele, and you will get a percentage of everything they do. And, if you still want to sell on the side, you can do that too."

It sounded like a good position. I was excited that someone had recognized the hard work I was doing, so I jumped at the opportunity. Basically my job was to recruit more representatives to come into the business. When I look back on this phase of my career, I realize just what kind of people I had been working with. I didn't know it at the time, but now I realize that they were not what they seemed at first. In fact, one was a loan shark, one was a pot dealer, one was a bookie, and another was a bank robber. During this entire time I actually thought that as I was learning this whole new career I was recruiting the "cream of the crop." It was problematic to me that this motley crew was considered the "cream." Even my boss at the time wasn't morally sound.

MetLife was built on a foundation of something called the "debit system." Every week, agents would knock on people's doors and collect the premium for their insurance. The majority of their business was done that way, mostly dealing with low-income families. In those days, not many people bought large chunks of life insurance.

Shortly after I started working at MetLife, the company decided that they wanted to transition their business from this debit system to a more traditional way of conducting business. Debit, unless it was collected in person, would go off the books. We're talking about collecting a dollar, two dollars, or ten dollars a week from these clients. This was a very expensive business to keep on the books because they would pay their sales force a weekly fee to go out and collect these premiums. So they realized this model was not going to support their growth.

As the company was trying to change their business and get out of the "debit" paradigm, however, they had put a huge focus on hiring people like me. I didn't have the trappings of a law degree, let alone an undergraduate degree. Nonetheless, they wanted to attract people like me – young, charming, and eager to please – to get in front of other people and convince them to buy larger blocks of life insurance. The abbreviated pitch would go like this: "Can you afford $100 a week? If not, can you afford $1 a week?" Most people could easily afford the latter. So then, knowing they could set aside somewhere between $1-100, you knew there was the possibility for a sale. That's the business MetLife hired me to recruit people into.

Along with this group of young people looking to sell, MetLife also had old time debit agents. There were approximately 50 debit agents in my office at the time. We would maybe hire 20 new people a year, and one of the senior agents would literally keep a scorecard of our performance, hoping this new crop would trip up and fail. I had entered a pool of sharks! It was a tough and challenging new profession. I was just learning the ropes, and it was extremely frustrating, because the people I dealt with on a daily basis were drug dealers and bookies, not to mention the older men trying to knock me and the other new recruits down.

I knew there had to be more out there than just this craziness. I was toiling away at an unsatisfying job while barely keeping my head above water. I would talk to other people at industry meetings who were also in the life insurance industry but who were working with other types of clients, and it sounded wonderful. That was the kind of work I wanted to do, and I was determined to find it.

On My Own, Paddling a Small Boat in a Large Stream

In October 1976 I was 22 years old and had just moved out of my mother's apartment. I was only taking home $215 a week, but I managed to get by. I found an apartment, which I shared with a roommate, and I also had a car. Meanwhile, to learn more about my industry, I would go to meetings run by an organization called the Life Underwriters Association of New York. Underwriting is the process that a large financial service provider such as a bank, insurer, or investment house uses to assess a customer's eligibility to receive their products – whether equity capital, insurance, mortgage, or credit. At these meetings I'd hear stories about incredibly successful people in the life insurance industry. I was working so hard to take home $15,000 a year, and these guys were making that in one month. I wanted to get to that level, but I knew I wouldn't be able to if I stayed in my current job.

At these meetings, some of the guys told stories about the uses of life insurance that I had never even dreamed of before. They were working with high-ticket items and their clients were buying millions of dollars in life insurance. At one of these meetings I met an older gentleman named Harold. I told him I was currently working at MetLife and not entirely happy with my job. He told me that he worked at a company called Home Life and that I should meet with the people who ran his agency.

This was one of the first times in my career that I realized how important networking is, because, before I knew it, I was meeting with one of the partners, Joe. During my interview with Joe, I saw all these pictures on his wall of him with people like Gerald Ford and Henry Kissinger – people that he had insured because of a relationship he had with NBC. I was immediately sold – I needed to work there!

This was in January 1978, and after a few more interviews they offered me a position. Home Life was known as the home of Planned Estates. Compared to MetLife, which was the largest insurance company in the world at that time, Home Life was this tiny New York based company with a much smaller sales force, and was eventually bought by Phoenix, a larger insurance company. However, what Home Life lacked in size, they made up in reputation. Everyone who worked there was bright and articulate, and as I stepped into their office, I knew I'd found the right place for me.

Ambitious and not afraid of hard work, I started to think I could do something bigger and more significant in my new job. However, I soon faced a similar problem to the one I had at MetLife: Home Life, too, asked me to move up to management, where I would hire people like myself to join the firm. I still didn't have any clients, and I was just trying to survive. What could I do? I already had my foot in the door in the field in which I wanted to work, so I went for it. I took the job in management and tried to think of it as a learning experience. I wanted to know as much about the industry as I could.

At the time, Home Life had just bought a franchise from a company called Physicians Planning Services, an organization where physicians at Columbia Presbyterian and other hospitals around the city could get a loan to help pay bills in a practice or residency. There were loan programs, discount programs, group insurance by mail, travel services – all kinds of concierge services designed to help physicians. I knew they would be great clients for me. This was designed as an entry vehicle to get in front of doctors in NYC. When I started recruiting people, I explained that this was a good marketing tool to help them build a clientele.

I began my recruiting at Columbia, NYU, Trinity College and

Williams College. I would go to these college campuses as a recruiter to try to get people to come into our insurance company. It was a great experience for me because the more I did it, the more confident I felt in relating to these younger people, who saw me in a leadership role.

While I was doing all of this planning for physicians, I started to think about the bigger picture: investment strategies, tax shelters, and other opportunities in the world of finance. That's when I decided to get my Series 6 certification and my Certified Financial Planning designation.

At that time, the Bank of New York chairman was on the board of Home Life, and the question that was circulating around was this: Can top sales people at Home Life provide financial planning for the clients at the custom banking division of the Bank of New York? It was a beautiful possibility – Bank of New York had the clients and the relationships, we had the expertise. It made sense to pool our resources and share the revenue.

A Mentorship For the Ages

When I found Home Life, I was introduced to a man named Tom Costello. Sometimes you meet a person who has the ability to change your life. Tom and I bonded right away. He was Joe's partner. He was an ex-NFL player, a former linebacker for the Giants, and he was making a whopping $250,000 a year. He always knew what to say, how to dress, had a great sense of humor, and more connections than you can imagine. What I thought would be a mere employee/employer relationship turned out to be a lifelong friendship. Tom eventually became my partner, my closest friend, and my daughter's godfather.

Tom taught me how to sell and what it meant to be a counselor and advisor. He taught me to not put up with people's B.S., whether it was a nasty know-it-all accountant or a client wasting my time. To this day I still seek Tom's counsel, as he does mine.

At Home Life, Tom convinced the company's top officers to bankroll a joint venture with the Bank of New York. We created a situation where we had a trust and estate attorney, an equity advisor, a pension consultant, and an MBA CPA running all the financial plans. Unfortunately though, this collaboration didn't succeed because the Bank of New York advisors at several branches saw us as a threat to their clients – they thought that we were going to take assets away from them.

At that point, we were trying to sell our financial plan for $5,000, but discovered that most people did not want to pay that much for such a plan. I remember meeting with a guy who had a huge tax problem. His biggest problem was that he was making a lot of money. He was 62 years old, a rubber trader, and was paying huge taxes and didn't know how to reduce them. I knew the answer was something called a Defined Benefit Pension Plan, but he didn't want to pay the fee for a financial plan.

I took a step back, swallowed my pride, and called him a week later. I said, "Forget the fee. Let's just fix your tax problem." I went to see him, installed a Defined Benefit Pension plan where he committed to putting away $100,000 a year every year for himself to retire, and he bought life insurance for a premium of $30,000 a year. It was the biggest sale and the biggest client I'd ever had at that point in my career.

Preparing for Change

In 1989, Tom asked me to move into his office on Central Park South. We started out with a 75/25 partnership, and eventually became 50/50 partners. I learned quickly that for me this business wasn't about charging people fees for financial planning – at its heart, it's about getting the clients to trust you and coming up with a solution together for their problems. It's not creating a financial plan that's the hard part; it's actually implementing that financial plan so that your clients get the most out of their assets.

After several years of working together Tom sat me down and said that it was time; he was finally done with the business and ready to retire. "Paul, you don't need me anymore," he said. "Also, I'm financially independent now and don't need or want to work anymore." We worked out a deal, and in 1993 I formed my own new company, Capital Estate Advisors.

The Only Constant in Life

All of these early experiences – personal and professional – have made me into what I describe as a realistic optimist. Someone smarter than me once said, "The only constant in life is change." Life is always going to throw curve balls at you. My job – which had become my true life's work – was to help my clients be ready for whatever comes their way, so they can sleep well at night and live the life they want, and not have to compromise on their dreams.

We'll return to this topic later on – specifically what it takes to ensure that your portfolio is keeping you well balanced and "bulletproof" for life's uncertainties. But first I want to talk to you about another important topic: Trust.

Whether a friendship, family relationship, or business connection, every strong bond is built on trust. Without it there is nothing to hold the relationship together. With it, you can do great things.

Trust is built and maintained overtime—usually by many small actions. As Warren Buffett once said, and I agree: "it takes 20 years to build a reputation and five minutes to ruin it."

Let's look closely at how trust plays out when it comes to finding the right partner to manage your assets and help guide your financial future.

"These woods are lovely, dark, and deep, but I have promises to keep and miles to go before I sleep."

— *Robert Frost*

3

Trust: The Essentials of Working with Other People's Money

At its core, my job is handling other people's money. Make no mistake – this requires a lot more work than a bank teller cashing your checks and counting out crisp bills. I handle entire fortunes. As such, clients' money isn't so much in my hands as it is balancing on my shoulders. Throughout my career as a Financial Advisor, I've learned how to treat my clients' money not just as I would my own, but better. If I make a mistake with my own money, it only affects me. If I make a mistake with someone else's, it will affect them, their family, and ultimately my professional reputation. Needless to say, I treat this aspect of my job with the utmost care.

Like any long-term relationship – personal or professional – the bond between you and your advisor must be based on mutual trust. I need my clients to feel comfortable trusting me with their money. This is a relationship really based on mutual appreciation and open communication. I really make people's money work for them, and that understanding needs to be established immediately before we start making any big plans or investments together.

Unfortunately, some financial professionals abuse this trust. We have seen countless horror stories plastered on the front page of the New York Times and various evening news stations about celebrities, athletes, and average Joes alike who have handed over their fortunes to someone they thought was working in their best interests, only to discover months or even years later that their money had been embezzled or squandered away. One of the most recent visible examples of this is the Bernie Madoff scandal. For a quick refresher, Madoff is a former stockbroker, investment advisor, and the former chairman of the NASDAQ stock market. He has also admitted to operating a Ponzi scheme that is now considered to be the largest financial fraud operation in U.S. history. Not only did Madoff ruin his own life by using his clients' money fraudulently and for decades living luxuriously off their money and winding up in jail for life, but he also ruined the lives of his co-workers, clients, and his own family members. Essentially, everyone in his financial sphere of influence was guilty of collusion in this massive debacle, whether or not they had actively participated in it.

The Madoff scheme is certainly an extreme example, but a cautionary tale nonetheless. The sheer evil behind Madoff's actions, rare as it is in an industry that has many fine and caring professionals in it, has understandably affected people who are on the verge of entrusting their money to a new advisor. I encourage you to do your research, feel out the relationship, and if you sense that anything is even slightly wrong, don't hesitate to speak up—or walk away and look elsewhere. After all, it's your life, not just your life savings, on the line.

A Narrow Escape into a New Life

Many of my clients are meticulous about their money, and with good reason. One that sticks out in my mind, and that has indelibly etched his story on my heart, is my client Tony. To fully understand Tony, though, we first have to go back in time.

It was the early 1930's and the Great Depression was in full swing. Tony was just a little boy, living a hardscrabble life in the Bronx. Packed into a one-family home were his parents, his four siblings, and his aunt and uncle. Tony's father was narrowly making ends meet, and his mother worked sporadically at the local Laundromat. His aunt had a slew of health problems, and his uncle was an alcoholic, so whatever little money Tony's parents were able to bring home was immediately spent on frugal suppers for him and his siblings and healthcare costs. When he was old enough, Tony picked up a paper route and each morning before school he would ride around his neighborhood on a second-hand bicycle, tossing papers on people's front lawns.

While Tony liked this little taste of independence, as well as the small collection of pocket change he was accruing, he would show up to school exhausted and haggard. Though most children in those days were far from having new clothes or new backpacks each year, Tony was picked on for his newspaper ink stained fingers and for nodding off during class. He was also one of the shortest kids in his class, and had to wear his older brother's hand-me-down trousers that were way too big on him, even with the bottoms cuffed three times.

One spring morning, just as Tony was rounding the last few houses on his paper route, he felt surprisingly energized. The sun was shining, and it almost seemed like there was a glimmer of hope on the horizon that the hard times for his family would turn around. His pockets jangled with coins as he pumped his legs on his bicycle and tossed the last few papers of the day. Just as he was about to make his way to school, a group of five older kids stopped him in his tracks. The older boys were on their bicycles, surrounded Tony, and began chasing him through the streets. They hurled offensive slurs at him, calling his family "dirty immigrants" and making rude comments about his mother, his aunt, and his two sisters.

Tony knew he should have just pedaled on, ignored their hurtful words, and make his way to school where he'd be under the watchful and sympathetic eye of the faculty, but his ego got the best of him. He didn't want to lose face in front of these bullies, so he tried yelling insults right back at them. Unfortunately, Tony's bicycle wheel hit a rock and knocked him off onto the street. The older boys wasted no time. They jumped off their bicycles and pummeled him, smashing his bicycle with a nearby trashcan, and stole the hard-earned money he kept in his pockets. He was left in the middle of the street with a broken bicycle, a broken nose, and a near-broken spirit.

Just as Tony felt completely defeated and was about to drag himself home with his tail between his legs, he remembered what his parents told him, that school was the most important thing, and that getting an education would be the only way to make yourself a better life. So Tony picked himself up, brushed himself off, left his bicycle on the side of the road, and walked the rest of the way to school. Though he was profoundly shaken up and even more upset that his hard-earned money was stolen from him, he was determined to not let a few bullies hold him back.

Let's jump back to present day. This brave little boy grew up, got married, had two children, and established an extremely successful construction business in Queens where he earned enough money to secure a net worth rivaling some of Hollywood's top movie stars. Even though an outsider might view his life as essentially perfect – with a multimillion-dollar fortune and a loving family, what more could one want? – Tony is still constantly brought back to that moment when those kids jumped him and took everything he had. Inside, he is still very much the same courageous yet scared little boy.

Tony has been my client for decades. His children are now grown and have their own families, and he is still married to his wife, Theresa. Unfortunately, he is also married to his job and his money. He has more than enough money to live comfortably for the rest of his life, but he still insists on working twelve-hour days. In doing so, he's managed to alienate almost all of his friends, and lately even his wife has begun to retreat from him, spending most of her time at their house in Connecticut while Tony toils away in New York.

Tony is the type of guy who won't let his money out of his sight for one second. He knows exactly how much he has at all times, down to the penny. One day I got a call from him and he was frantic. Tony had always been high-strung, but his tone on that day implied an unnamable catastrophe. I sat at my desk, gearing up for what he was about to drop on me. He said he had looked at his statement and that he knew what he paid for his Apple, Visa, Wal-Mart and Johnson & Johnson stocks.

"Paul, the statements I have are all different," he complained. "Why is that?" Clearly he wanted to know if I had been misquoted or fooling him. I explained that because there were multiple purchases of the same stocks with dividends being reinvested, all at different prices, he was looking at statements showing average costs, not his one-time original stock buy.

I've had my fair share of scrupulous clients, but none that have come anywhere close to Tony. I realized, though, that this sudden questioning of my integrity wasn't a failure of character on his part. This was a manifestation of Post-Traumatic Stress Disorder. Every time he felt out of control, it must have brought him back to being beaten up and mugged.

Know Your Clients and Know Yourself

After Tony confronted me about the acquisition costs, I hadn't heard from him or his wife, Theresa, for two weeks. I knew something was up, because I would hear from the guy constantly, and then all of a sudden, nothing. I held off calling, because I knew how they were. If something was bothering them, they'd have to broach the subject on their own terms. Sure enough, after two silent weeks, I received a phone call.

It was his wife Theresa. She said, "Paul, I don't want you to think we've been avoiding you, we have not been. We're so busy with things and have so much to talk to you about." I asked her, "Theresa, is this about the acquisition cost of his stock?" Silence.

I continued, "If you have to question my integrity after working twenty years with you and your family, then I must be missing something." She said, "I would never question it. I know exactly how you feel about us because I feel the same way about you. Theresa said, "Tony is afraid to call you because he insulted you. He thinks you are angry and won't talk to him."

Tony, this rough and tough child of the streets, was too intimidated to call me. I told Theresa, "Stop. I will call him right now and fix this!"

There was no question – I had to adjust my communication style for them. I had thought I was being transparent enough with his account, but sometimes you need to be reminded to slow down and start from the beginning, even with clients that you've been working with for years. No matter how well you think you know your clients, they're bound to surprise you, and the most successful financial professionals will know how to roll with the punches.

Keep Tony and his family in mind – he's going to pop up a few more times throughout the book. When you've worked with so many different people for as long as I have, you pick up a lot of stories, trials-and-errors, and neuroses along the way. Not to mention a keen appreciation of the often dysfunctional emotional connection people have when it comes to money – making it, saving it, investing it, and giving it away.

Planning for Life's Unexpected Moments

One aspect of my job I am most passionate about is helping people who are in unique, and sometimes challenging, circumstances. One of these clients is Gary. Gary served in Iraq and came back completely paralyzed from the waist down – not to mention emotionally damaged. Upon returning home, Gary moved back in with his parents – he was only twenty-three at the time and had been dating a young woman named Doris, but they weren't ready to move in together yet, especially since Gary's new physical limitations required extra care and extra costs.

Once he was settled, Gary enrolled in a local college on his GI bill and began working towards getting a degree in social work. While he loved the intellectual challenge that this academic setting provided him, he knew his medical costs were still a huge financial burden to his parents, who were nearing retirement age. He was also ready to propose to Doris, but was hesitant because they couldn't yet afford their own place – let alone renovate one to be wheelchair-accessible.

Gary knew it was a long shot, but he started buying lottery tickets. At the end of every week, he'd buy a Powerball ticket and some scratch-offs. Against all odds, he wound up winning millions of dollars on Powerball! The first thing Gary did was purchase an engagement ring. The second thing he did, as per his parents' sage advice, was arrange a meeting with a financial advisor – me.

We worked together to determine a budget for a house, and then I helped him get in touch with a great real estate broker, who found him a fantastic, accessible house on Long Island. Gary could have chosen any financial advisor to help him, but I'm pretty sure he chose me because of my sincerity. My passion for helping him make the most of his new situation was apparent. He and Doris were young and in love, didn't have any children, and now had a solid foundation on which to build their new lives. I saw it as an artist sees a blank canvas; the raw potential was inspiring.

After I helped him find his house, Gary began to see me as more than somebody who was just going to invest his money. He could see that I was taking a genuine interest in his life, not merely looking for a way to make money from his predicament. Then, just as he and Doris were settling into their new home, they quickly discovered a sneaking issue right in their backyard. Their property was overrun with hemp dogbane, a type of weed that emits a toxic sap that is poisonous to animals and can burrow its roots six feet into the ground! Originally, Native Americans used the plant to make rope and clothing, but today it's a weed that decimates crops and can harm humans and animals.

This was an especially difficult problem since Gary was in his wheelchair, and could not perform even the most cursory landscaping tasks. Not to mention that any time you cut the branches, the dogbane plants exuded a sap that irritated skin. Plus, it required a lot more than a few snips from hedge-clippers – it required digging up full roots. However, I took this on as part of my relationship with him, and with my help, Gary and I were able to negotiate a deal with one company. Within a few months, their dogbane problem was completely gone.

When you hire me, I do a lot more than tell you how to spend your money – I stick around until the bitter end, making sure that you and your family are comfortable, happy, and free of any unwanted garden pests!

Starting Over in Your Later Years

One of my clients, Marilyn, had a husband who died many years before, and she'd been running his business for a long time. She was making a good living until a larger company bought out their company, and ultimately let her go in the re-organization process. This would be difficult for anyone, but the fact that she got laid off when she was in her seventies presented a whole different challenge. She wanted to keep working, but what would she do? Sadly, this is an all too common issue among senior citizens these days. Like many people who are forced to make a major life change, she was petrified.

I sat down with her and she said, "Paul, here are my assets, here's is what I'm used to making, and here's what I need to live on. Can we make it work?" I was impressed with her preparedness and self-awareness. She knew exactly what she had and what she wanted: if only all of my clients were this clear! I did the math and determined that it would be possible for her to live a comfortable life without ever having to work again.

I said, "There are three things you should know. Number 1: You're in good shape – relax. Number 2: As long as you don't open up a bar or a club, you'll be fine. Number 3: What is your heart telling you? What would you like to do that you've never done?" She said, "I'd love to travel to South America." So I said, "Do it. Book a month and go to Brazil. You deserve it."

She had three million dollars, lived on Long Island, and didn't have a mortgage. She was actually in a lot better shape than many people who find themselves in similar situations. On the flip side, there are many people out there who are one or two paychecks away from disaster, yet don't know it. You hear about people who have worked as executives their whole lives, lose their jobs for one reason or another, and suddenly find themselves with no savings left. Unemployment runs out quicker than you'd think, and sometimes it's hard to find a job, even as a greeter at Wal-Mart.

Personalizing Your Financial Plan

People will often say, "Paul, be straight with me. How much money do I need to be truly comfortable? Two million? Five million?" To me, being truly comfortable is not about two or five; it's not the number that matters. Living a comfortable life is not even about the total value of your assets. It's really about the best income you can generate from those assets. Suppose a client with three million dollars comes to me with a portfolio generating $90,000 a year, but they need $140,000 to live their current lifestyle. That's a problem. Suppose a different client needs the same $140,000 to live on, and has the same net worth but we have gotten it to generate $180,000 a year in interest and dividends—a major difference!

Many clients do come to me with the same amount of money, yet the way in which I approach their assets and portfolios will be extremely different, since each client has his or her own unique needs and desires. No two plans will ever be completely alike. In the end, too, it is not about the total of all your assets, liquid and otherwise. How we structure and balance your assets really have a lot to do with your attitude towards money, how you want to live your life, and the compromises you're willing to make.

In the following chapter, I delve deeper into what exactly I believe it means to be truly "rich." The answers might surprise you.

"If we command our wealth, we shall be rich and free; if our wealth commands us, we are poor indeed."

— *Edmund Burke*

4

Rich: Getting Past Illusions and Defining Wealth in a Whole New Way

What does it mean to be rich? At what point can you consider yourself wealthy? Is there a magic number? In a way, that's like asking, "What's the meaning of life?" Wealth is an extremely subjective topic, one that inspires many varied answers, and makes many people uncomfortable. More often than not, when people ask me, I turn the question back to them. I understand this can be frustrating, which is why I've devoted this chapter to explaining this paradox. Through real life examples from some of my clients, you'll come to understand that wealth comes in all shapes and sizes. Not all of these examples are positive – far from it. I offer these stories to show you that merely having a significant net worth doesn't necessarily equate to "being wealthy."

Furthermore, in my experience, many people have delusions when it comes to their money. Even some of the smartest, most rational people tend to get confused, angry and upset when faced with financial matters. This is because emotions are inherently tied to one's fortune. I like to think of a portfolio as a teenager on the cusp of leaving for college. You've done all you could do to raise them well, make sure they get the best high school education they can, make sure they stay nourished and relatively clean, and instill in them strong morals and values that can see them through life. As difficult as it can be to loosen your hold, you know you will have to relinquish some of that control. It's usually in your child's best interest to go to college so they can

39

learn things that you, their parents, aren't able to teach them. Think of "college" in this case as your financial advisor. You might mean well with your money, and you want to do all you can to protect it – sometimes to the point of suffocation – but ultimately you will have to come to terms with the fact that you might not be the best person to manage it.

If you fall into this category – which most people do – don't feel discouraged. Frankly most people don't know how to intelligently manage their money. This is why my profession exists – so that you can have an expert working for you. Everyone has his or her own expertise. When my car needs a tune-up, I go to a mechanic. When I have a toothache, I go to a dentist. When you need help managing your money, you go to a financial advisor.

I know people who keep hundreds of thousands of dollars or more in their checking accounts. This is the modern-day equivalent of keeping stacks and stacks of bills underneath your mattress. Listen, I get it – people are scared and all they want is to be able to see their money and know it's there when they need it. Some of them have immigrant parents who came to the United States with a few coins in their pocket and worked their entire lives to secure their fortune. This money could be working for them, but they're terrified of losing it so they let it sit there in the bank, essentially collecting dust. Actually, it's worse than collecting dust: inflation is devaluing each dollar like piranhas nipping at it tiny bite by tiny bite until it's half gone.

You might think accumulating dollars makes you "rich," but I view being wealthy as bringing one's portfolio up to its full potential. Much like your teenage child, if your money just sits at home, it'll never develop into all it can be.

The Dependent Child and Your Portfolio

Speaking of parents and children, the relationship that exists between wealthy parents and their dependent children can often pose a problem. For one example, let's focus on my clients Dave and Barbara. Like several of my other clients, Dave owns his own business and has built it into something of an empire, acquiring a number of assets in the process. Barbara also works in the business. Dave doesn't have to work anymore, but he chooses to because he wants to remain active. She is 68 and he is 71. They have four kids, all in their mid-30s, and two of them still live at home. Their daughter Sarah, who doesn't work, has a live-in boyfriend who works as a part time chef. Their son Mark has a girlfriend who doesn't work. Mark originally had aspirations of opening and running an Italian restaurant, but these half-formed plans ultimately tanked when he couldn't acquire a liquor license.

Like many doting parents, Dave and Barbara love their kids more than anything. However, their love for them is sometimes so overwhelming that they become blind to their faults, and more of enablers than parents. Finally, a major problem jolted Dave and Barbara out of their reverie and allowed them to understand just how poor their son Mark's decision-making had become.

For Mark's birthday, Dave and Barbara bought him a brand new Ferrari. Now, that's what I call a birthday present! Unfortunately, the joy was short-lived. After just one week with the Ferrari, Mark took it on a joyride with his friend Tim. To no one's surprise, Tim – who had recently been released from rehab and was carrying an expired driver's license – crashed and totaled the car. The cost was astronomical. Not only was the $185k for the car flushed down the drain, but also the property damage that the accident caused nearly totaled an additional $850k!

Typically when Mark would get himself into trouble – which was often – Dave would step in, clean up his messes, and hope nothing worse happens the next time. This time there really was nothing that could have been worse – unless someone had died in the crash. So Dave--with Barbara's wholehearted agreement—put his foot down and told Mark to figure it out for himself. Aside from the fact that this incident, to me, sounded more like the actions of a badly spoiled teenager rather than a thirty-something man, I knew right away I was dealing with a bad case of codependency. It wasn't just money that Mark was relying on his father and mother for – it was everything.

When Dave told me this, I knew that in my role as a financial advisor, I wasn't qualified to offer him any sort of legal counsel. Instead I did the only thing I could: I helped him find the best attorney possible.

After this dire situation was resolved, Dave and Barbara were forced to rethink their definition of "wealth." In truth, they both liked having two of their adult children live at home with their significant others. But now, seeing that their children were essentially taking advantage of them they had to determine just how much of the "purse-strings" they wanted to keep open to them. They began to appreciate that they had unknowingly kept them in an adolescent – if not infantile – state of dependency that was unhealthy and hampering their growth as fully functioning independent adults. Unfortunately, this is a far too common situation, one I see often. For Dave and Barbara, it took a near-tragedy to open their eyes. Getting an "education" is expensive! Thankfully it all worked out in the long run. But if this situation hits home, hopefully you will take their example to heart and make some serious changes—creating a more mature and "enriching" environment without the angst and guilt that comes from overindulging your children in a way that hampers their growth!

First Things First: Understanding How Much You Have

I mentioned previously that I have a number of clients who, like Tony, know exactly how much money they have at all times. Not all are like him, though. Some of my clients need some goading to even open their portfolios and see what's inside. In this regard, we have Sylvia, who came as a referral from an existing client. The first time I met Sylvia I went to her home in Huntington out on Long Island, New York. That afternoon, her daughter, Phyllis, was there to look after her. Sylvia, then 80, was spry, but her body wasn't in as good a shape as her mind. I had a lot of paperwork to carry, since this was our first meeting, so I packed it all into my big, black briefcase. When her daughter opened the door and led me in, Sylvia's first words to me were, "Oh, he's like a doctor – he's got a doctor bag. What are you going to do, give me an examination?" She was certainly a cheeky one!

Sylvia's husband Phil had recently passed away, and now she lived alone in this nice large house, which is why her daughter spent so much time with her. During that initial meeting she gave me full access to her accounts. Judging from her attitude, I thought I was going to discover that she had a comfortable yet modest portfolio. However, when I started going through everything, I quickly realized that she was sitting on a lot more than she had let on. I had to adjust my perspective and I realized that my initial impressions would have to be re-evaluated. I couldn't get through my first sentence before she interrupted me. Sylvia said, "Paul, this can't be. I don't have that kind of money." I said, "Sylvia, these are your statements – this is your account. You actually do have this money."

Can you believe it? She wasn't aware of how much money

she had. Maybe she hadn't been paying attention to her accounts since her husband passed, or maybe she was in some sort of denial that all this money was hers because it was too overwhelming to think about. Either way, it was one of the more bizarre moments I've had with any client. Usually I have to show people that they don't have as much money as they think they do – for Sylvia, it was the exact opposite.

Once Sylvia had come to terms with her fortune, she started taking a real interest in her portfolio. She would call me periodically, and the conversations were always the same. She'd say, "Paul, it's Sylvia." I'd say, "Hi, Sylvia. How are things going?" She'd say, "My money's working? Everything is going okay?" I'd say, "Yes," and she'd say, "Paul, tell me – are you REALLY watching it?" I'd say, "Yes, Sylvia. I'm really watching it." It was inspiring to me her taking an active interest in her finances. It seemed like she was finally getting excited about something since her husband died.

Some years after that initial meeting, Sylvia passed away. Before she died, though, I made sure she had a set plan for her beneficiaries. There was no question in her mind that she wanted to leave everything to her three daughters. Sometimes when I work with my deceased clients' children, or other beneficiaries, tension or personality clashes arise. This is understandable, since they just lost someone close to them, but some of them become hostile and start arguing with me. Fortunately, Sylvia daughters weren't like this. Clearly, Sylvia's lively personality was so strong that it transferred over to her offspring, and it was a great pleasure to work with her smart, funny daughters after she died.

Sylvia gave me a drawing that she had done as a teenager. I think of her often. She was a talented and accomplished artist, and I'm proud to have worked with her while she was still alive.

Real Estate as an Investment

While having a portfolio like Sylvia's, chock full of liquid assets, is great, it is far from the only measure of one's wealth. Real estate is another tangible asset that needs to be factored in. If mom and dad retire and plan on moving out of their single family home to a condo in Fort Lauderdale, it's not uncommon for them to turn the deed over to their young adult children who may be first starting families of their own. However, over the past ten years, some real estate properties have become like a thorn in many homeowners' side. Many properties have decreased tremendously in value, and real adjustments had to be made across the U.S., as well as in even the biggest real estate havens in the country, including the Hamptons, Manhattan, Florida, San Francisco and Las Vegas.

That being said, most people – myself included – still consider real estate a good investment, whether it's for appreciation potential, rental income, or having a home to pass down to your children and grandchildren. As for the latter benefit, though, it has become dangerous to view your living space as an asset because the market can turn at any minute. Nonetheless, I certainly do take my clients' homes into account when determining their overall assets, whether it's their residence, a vacation home, a condo, or commercial real estate properties.

Finding Your Financial Comfort Zone

There's an old joke about a man witnessing a minor car accident, in which someone is hit by a cab and is knocked down. The witness runs up to him and asks, "Are you comfortable?" The accident victim, dirty and bruised, looks up and answers: "Well, I can't complain – I make a living!"

All joking aside, I believe "comfortable" means that you have enough money being generated in your portfolio to live life on your own terms. To me that is the ideal definition of "being rich." If you know you can always generate $200k a year, you need $300k to live your life, and I can get you $150k in income and dividends to spend effectively to make up the difference on your portfolio, are you comfortable in this scenario? I would say you are. Very.

Too many people live their lives thinking, "If only I had a million dollars, five million dollars, ten million dollars – then I'd be rich!" Those numbers are essentially meaningless without taking many other factors into consideration. Even celebrities and top earning CEOs will fall into the trap of comparing themselves to someone who may have more and believe they don't have enough. Typically, the more a person has to begin with, the more they want. This is because their wants become more sophisticated and they have become accustomed to a certain lifestyle. This happened to me, after I graduated from college and began working in life insurance. I remember thinking that if I could just make $50k a year, I'd be set. Once I reached that $50k my "happy number" turned to $100k, and so on. It's understandable, but it can lead you down a dangerous path as life's journey continues.

The smartest clients I have begin to devise a new and improved plan as they get older. Perhaps retirement is looming in the distance, and they want to start adjusting their lifestyle so that when the time does come to stop working it's not so much of a shock.

They figure out how many cars or houses they really need or want. In this instance, what most of them realize is that they want to be able to spend more time with their families. When the time does come to downsize, they've pre-determined the best situation, the plan that will keep them the most comfortable financially and psychologically. For some, it's about moving out of the big suburban house and leaving behind the yard, pool, and other high-maintenance amenities for a smaller place in the city where they may have a more reasonable overhead and also have access to some cultural activities and venues and spend more time with friends. For others, it could be about moving to a warmer climate, or perhaps traveling more often. Wherever they determine they will feel most comfortable is where I will help them go.

The Upside to Downsizing

Let's talk about downsizing a bit more in-depth. It's something my clients ask me about a lot, especially as they get older and their children start "flying the coop." However, they may not necessarily want to downsize just yet. Many couples enjoy being "empty-nesters" because now that the kids are out of the house, they can regain some of the old spark that brought them together in the first place. They may have finally become more financially secure in their careers, and want to enjoy what they have while they're still able. They may start to go on "dates" again with each other, or take trips they weren't able to take when the kids were around. Some even humorously embrace their so-called "mid-life crises" together and make a larger purchase such as the motorcycle they always wanted or finally redo the kitchen. I can, and have, helped many clients do those things and more. For them, it's not about wanting to live extravagantly – it's more about using their earnings to enjoy this next chapter in their lives, as a couple and as individuals. This part – identifying interests and integrating them into their lives – is a lot of fun!

On the other hand, I do have the clients who want to downsize years before they really need to. They decide they don't necessarily need that other car they were considering, or are interested in selling the second one they already own. Maybe instead of redoing the kitchen, they would rather move into a smaller home or apartment that costs less and/or requires less maintenance. I sometimes wonder, though, if some people really want to downsize, or if for them it's more about coming to terms with the reality of what they have. My job is to establish that reality. I know that whenever clients ask me about downsizing there's usually a current and good, if not always immediately apparent, reason for it, such as they've had to take a pay cut, had to take out a second mortgage on their home, or suffered an illness or another one of the "3 D's": death, divorce, or disaster.

Transcending the Role of the Advisor

Hopefully, through the few examples I've provided so far, you are able to get a sense of how I work. I also hope it surprises you. Perhaps you previously thought of an advisor as someone who just sits across a desk and punches numbers into a calculator. I think now you'll see that it's less about crunching or "punching" numbers and far more about understanding my clients' current lifestyles, family succession, dreams, desires, and yes, their fears.

A few weeks ago, I met with a client named Richard at his attorney's office. I went there to be supportive and informative. He was in the process of redoing his wills and trust documents because he and his wife had recently divorced. Sitting down to figure out those logistics is never easy, but it becomes especially difficult and painful when you're forced to recalibrate your heirs and other financial factors. I was moved that Richard asked me to come with him, because I knew that meant he felt comfortable enough with me for me to be in the room. When I got there, and he and his attorney started parsing through his assets for the will and the trust, he told me he actually wanted me to be the sole trustee.

I was shocked. I asked him, "Richard, are you sure?" He said that he felt that I would be the one person who would best carry out his wishes. Of course, it would be my duty to then take the money and distribute it to his children, and among certain charities we discussed in the meeting, but it was still a big decision for him to make. I accepted this responsibility with pride, and was honored that he entrusted me with such an important aspect of his life.

Moving Forward

Over the years, I've discovered the surprising fact that most people are terrified of making a mistake with their money. For some, just the idea of this happening is enough to bring on an anxiety attack. This is why they seek me out. They want to hand the decision-making over to me so they don't even have to think about it. However, when people relinquish all control, they also give up the right to protest when things don't always go their way. If you say to your hairdresser, "Do whatever you think," and they chop off too much of your hair, you really don't have a right to complain. Likewise, tell the chef at a restaurant "surprise me" and hopefully it will be a delicious dish – but there are no guarantees!

My best clients, the ideal clients, are those who can trust me to take care of their money, while still taking an interest in their portfolios. It's all about establishing a balance.

So, how does one define wealth? Clearly, coming up with an answer that works for everyone is tricky, but separating people from their illusions – and encouraging them to take risks – is trickier. As a financial advisor, it's my job to hold up the mirror of reality and help people come to terms with their financial situation. I don't do this to discourage them – rather I want to teach my clients how to live comfortable, happy lives within their means, without putting their fortune at risk. I encourage my clients to strive for more, within attainable, well-thought-out goals. In fact, creating small goals and meeting them incrementally is the perfect way to get positive results as well as boost their confidence.

In the next chapter I'm going to delve deeper into some specific areas of expertise a financial advisor should have, and how working with an experienced professional will give you a major advantage in making your money work for you.

"Price is what you pay, value is what you get."

— *Warren Buffett*

5

Relationships: When to Fully Trust Your Advisor's Expertise

As I explained in an earlier chapter, my parents treated me like an adult from a very young age. As a result, I became privy to the realities of the world much earlier than most of my childhood friends. My father's failing health and my mother's constant concerns about him and about money taught me that life was filled with challenges and turmoil, but also that each day was precious. Many children have the luxury of growing up without understanding the stresses behind money, but I had no such filter.

I remember sometimes feeling too old for my age, as if I was already a grown-up living in a child's body. That made me especially frustrated when my father lectured me. He'd say, "Paul, don't you know that you can't get something for nothing?" He was trying to impart some fatherly wisdom, but I listened begrudgingly. It wasn't until I was a little older and finally starting my career that his words began to make sense to me. In fact I still keep this simple but profound tenet in the back of my mind whenever I take on a new client, or find myself in a predicament with an existing client—everything in life has a cost, and if you're not giving a lot you can't expect to get a lot.

In virtually every business based on a client-consultant relationship, questions or disagreements about fees may arise. Whether you're shopping for automotive repair or for the right financial advisor, my opinion is that if you only focus on what it's going to cost you instead of the benefits you will gain – whatever it is the expert is helping you repair – you are probably setting yourself up for a less than successful outcome.

Taking Care of Business

Let's return to our friends Tony and Theresa. When you have two people with such strong personalities, it's not too surprising when their children share some of the same character traits or idiosyncrasies. Tony and Theresa's two children, Michael and Emma, are just as strong-willed as their parents.

The whole stock purchase price debacle unearthed some lingering concerns for Tony, Theresa, and their family as a whole. And apparently Tony had been talking to his wife about taking their business elsewhere. Theresa called me up and said, "Paul, I told Tony that if he wants to take his money someplace else, I won't have any part of it." Basically, she gave Tony an ultimatum – either they stay under my advisement, or she would remove herself from the situation. She said, "Then I told Michael that he'd have to deal with his father on all financial matters because if we're not working with Paul, I quit. He was not very happy about that!"

Tony was also in the process of turning over some of his Coca Cola shares to his children. This is a common practice for many of my older clients – not only do they start perfecting their wills and securing their benefactors, but they also start transferring over shares, properties, and other assets. A decision of whether to gift low cost (low basis) assets to your children versus high costs (high basis) assets is a very personal decision that has to take into account certain specifics from the client's overall overall financial picture.

The Reality of Real Estate

Now let's check in on Dave, the father with the codependent adult children. Mark, his son, was getting money from his father's restaurant business. To the outsider looking in, Dave's business would seem to be thriving, but after sitting in on a few meetings with him, I quickly realized that it was actually in danger of crumbling.

What was happening was that Dave and his sons were partners in a side business – some clothing stores. Dave put up all the money to buy and build the properties, but this was based upon the stores generating positive cash flow and profits. Mark was supposed to return half of those profits to his dad. So far after three years Dave had not seen a penny.

One day, Dave emailed me to tell me that he and his son were closing on another deal. Mark had been buying a store out on Eastern Long Island that required $500,000 – from Dave. It was a never-ending list, and it changed every week. I also couldn't believe that Dave didn't know exactly what he was supposed to get in revenue from each property. With all this chaos, the fact that he had a somewhat functioning business was incredible.

Clearly this dysfunctional situation was due to the fact that his son was constantly breathing down his neck for money, and then squandering it away on too many projects. I sat Dave down and told him, "Dave, you're all over the place. You need to create a clear plan of what money is coming in and what money you're sending out. I will help you, but we need to clean this up."

In addition to being up front with him about his need for better organization, I strongly urged him to stop. He'd already put in over $3 million. The problem was that Dave was still so optimistic, and had so much faith in his son that he didn't even notice how many times he was proven wrong. Again, I found myself toeing a line – I was hired to advise him on his finances, but now personal matters were coming into play. I had to take a step back and evaluate the situation before saying something that could have compromised our professional relationship.

I finally said, "Dave, I admire your dedication to your family, so here's my suggestion: please don't spend another dime until the properties start to generate profits and you start to get some of your money back." I explained that this way he would still be able to support his son, but would also stop hemorrhaging money. Dave gave it some thought, came around, and agreed to change the way he conducted business with his son.

And Then There Was More

Unfortunately, Dave's son wasn't the only member of the family causing him stress. He was also involved with a partner that he did not trust or respect. The two of them were 50/50 partners in several furniture stores. They had been butting heads personally and professionally for years. Dave had decided he wanted OUT.

I knew I had to step in to save Dave from making any bigger mistakes. I reviewed expenses and revenue flow for the business and tried to find an intelligent exit strategy for Dave. It seemed like the best way to do this, without causing more problems than already existed, was to tackle it piece by piece. The best place to start, I thought, would be to value the inventory. It took weeks just to sort out this first step, from accounts payable to accounts receivable, to Goodwill, etc. Once we finally sorted it all out, Dave got his check and was happy.

Yes, this possibly was outside the scope of the financial advisor. However, I do get asked to counsel clients on various aspects of their business and quite often their personal affairs, which is not surprising because of the level of respect and trust between us.

Very often emotions can clutter the forest and ruin negotiations. That's where a knowledgeable third party can help find intelligent solutions that can satisfy everyone.

Two of my clients, Abe and Marvin, are brothers. Their real estate group owned undeveloped land that was zoned for residential construction in one of the most exclusive areas in East Hampton, NY.

This land had been inherited from their recently deceased father who had owned it for over 25 years. When you inherit a certain level of assets you may have to pay estate taxes based on the value of those assets. Generally speaking, taxes are due nine months subsequent to the death of their former owner.

Under certain guidelines those taxes can be and had been postponed for some years. Now the IRS wanted to get paid. My job was to figure out how to raise the money to pay those taxes and help structure a deal fair to both parties. Not all parcels were owned equally and only one of the brothers was my client. As an aside, a huge fight broke out between their respective CPAs and attorneys.

I was asked to intercede and mediate a negotiation with just the CPAs and myself in the room. What was important to me was that both brothers felt like they had gotten a fair deal. We found a way to pay the government and everyone moved on. We even toasted each other during a celebratory dinner.

There are several important messages here for clients. When you have a multi-year relationship with someone, as I did in the prior example, they are used to me going above and beyond for them. My advice is that you should know early in the relationship what you are paying for. If you ask your advisor to go above and beyond those expectations, you should also ask if there are additional fees.

There are differences between what one financial advisor will do and what another will do, just as how there are differences with how often you will meet, speak, etc. Here is where open communication can work wonders. It will eliminate any surprises...or at least decrease your chances for unpleasant ones! I believe that a one-size-fits-all policy is not reality. People have very different needs, issues, and expectations. The scope of these should determine the fee – not just the size of the account.

Father Knows Best

There's a commercial on TV for a large alternative money management company that drives me nuts. It says, "Ever think about what you're paying for your money management? If you're paying a percent in annual fees, it might not sound like much, but it adds up! If you come to us, there's no fee!" I'm very put off by that because, to me, that diminishes the work that I and so many other advisors do. This isn't a business where I'm sitting on my bed, in pajamas, looking at your portfolio on a laptop while I eat Doritos. I have an office and a family to support. I have people who work for me – they support my clients just as much as I do, and they too deserve to be fairly compensated. Managing money is not about doing it one day, and then it's all set for the year – every portfolio requires constant upkeep and sharp attention to detail.

My expertise is my ability to determine the best plan for my clients, execute it for them, and keep it working. I know that I am not right for everybody, and vice versa. For one thing, some people are delusional about business costs. One client didn't want to pay an annual fee for me to manage his portfolio. He said, "Why don't you just charge me every time there's a transaction? I'll pay that way."

After much protestation, I said, "Fine." I really wanted to use my father's words here and tell him that he "can't get something for nothing," but I resisted the lecture. He clearly thought he knew better. Then he started calling me regularly – "Buy me 500 shares of JP Morgan, buy me $100,000 worth of Apple, 500 shares of American Express," etc. etc. Finally, at the end of the quarter, I calculated how much he had paid me versus how much he would have had to pay if he went with my original plan. With his idea, he wound up paying three times the annual management fee he would have paid. Needless to say, when he saw the facts he switched to the annual charge.

I could have said nothing, and reaped the benefits, but I have a conscience. For me, it always comes down to integrity: earning and keeping people's trust. The only reason I let this guy do things his way for one quarter of the year was because he was so adamant that I was wrong and so insistent on doing it his way. The best "I told you so" moments usually come from people proving themselves wrong!

I hope this gives you a better idea of what to look for – and what to reasonably expect – from your financial advisor.

Next, we are going to talk about retirement. But brace yourself – my views on retirement may not be "politically correct." I don't believe in "retiring" the way most people think of it. I wish we had a better word for this third act of life, where you ideally will have an enormous cache of knowledge and insights to share from both your profession and your life—gifts that you should be well able to use to create a substantial income stream. So if you're ready to take a fresh look at retirement, turn the page.

"Life is like riding a bicycle. To keep your balance you must keep moving."

— *Albert Einstein*

6

Retirement: What Factors to Consider in Making This Very Personal Decision

Today retirement, in my opinion, has become an outdated concept for a great many of us. I include myself in the "no plans to ever retire" category. I think there are compelling reasons to stay in the game. Perhaps the game is a different one than what you've been doing most of your life, but I can tell you this: what I am proposing doesn't involve early bird specials in Florida. Not that there's anything wrong with that, if it brings you what you feel you want in your own personal Act Three.

So please, let me rewind and start from the beginning. If you don't agree now, maybe you will by the end of this chapter.

As an estimated 76 million Baby Boomers – those born in the United States between 1946 and 1964 – head down the road towards those traditional "retirement years" right now, it's a fact that many, if not most, are quickly realizing they may not be as prepared to stop working as they once thought they would be.

Of course the prospect of never working again is attractive. Who hasn't thought about leaving behind their 9-to-5 grind, hanging up their work outfits, and finally making time for hobbies, trips, and spending time with their families? Of course you deserve some time off or time out after working for the better part of your life. However, these hobbies and trips cost money – money that you may have, but which, once used, may not be coming in again. And aside from extra trips, just living your usual day-to-day life costs money. Money keeps the lights and heat on in your house. It keeps you and your family fed, and keeps the IRS at bay – alas, you can't forget about those property taxes!

A number of new clients I met with were on the brink of retirement. They told me they were sure that once they stopped going to work, their living costs would be much lower. They were mostly thinking about commuting costs and other daily expenses directly related to their jobs. They also said they felt fairly sure they had accumulated enough of a nest egg to be able to live without the steady income. What most of them did not take into account was just how much they would have to keep spending day-to-day, month-to-month, and year-to-year. This includes not only everyday expenses such as food and the roof over their head, but also larger expenses such as medical bills, which can burn a big hole in your savings. They also didn't factor in the cost of the leisure travelling they wanted to do, plus more frequent trips to see the kids and grandkids, and, for many, the continuing help they were giving their adult children and grandchildren, which was going to also continue taking a big chunk out of their principal. These funds would have to be replenished somehow, or drastic changes in their lifestyle or spending habits would need to be made.

Maybe you've heard the phrase, "A parent can take care of six kids, but six kids can't take care of mom or dad." A few years ago, I had a client who was nearing retirement age. Like many others, he was convinced he had his entire retirement mapped out. He wasn't wrong. I checked his finances and everything looked like it was in order. Between his wife, who had retired several years before, and he himself, they had plenty of money. However, about a year into his retirement, his 45-year-old son – who had triplet toddlers – fell on hard times. It was now up to my client and his wife to support them financially until they got back on their feet. Suddenly my client's nest egg didn't seem so ample anymore, and he and his wife had to re-enter the work force to provide for their son. They didn't return to their former jobs and salaries, but they did take part-time jobs that were closer to home so they could supplement their income and avoid draining their retirement funds.

Years ago, in a time before cell phones and email, the majority of the American working class found jobs in factories, ran farms, or worked in any number of other jobs that required physical labor. That was why the ultimate annuity, Social Security, started in the first place. People used to work so hard that their bodies broke down; at age 65 most people needed to retire because they physically couldn't work anymore. Social Security they received from the government would cover at least a good portion of their living expenses – if they lived frugally.

In retirement, since you aren't working, you need something else to fill those eight or more hours of your day and now instead of two days free you have seven. Maybe you go to the movies, go shopping at the mall, or take up hobbies. In any case, you're going to spend more money. The misconception is that in retirement you will have fewer expenses when in fact you will have more – especially if you are healthy and want to live a fulfilling life.

Pension Tension

Company pension plans were once the centerpiece of most people's anticipated retirement income. A pension plan is a type of retirement plan, usually tax sheltered, in which your employer makes contributions into a pool of funds set aside for each employee's future benefit. This pool of funds is then invested on the employee's behalf, allowing the employee to receive benefits upon retirement – either in the form of a monthly check or sometimes one lump sum. In the past, it was your boss's responsibility to pay for your pension plan, just as it was his job to make sure you got paid each month. Now many of those pension plans – as well as their parent corporations – no longer exist, and have been replaced by 401k plans. It is now largely up to employees themselves to fund their retirement. Each month you can put part of your salary into your 401k, and if your boss wants to do this, he or she can decide at the end of the year to either match that contribution or provide a percentage of what you've put in.

In other words, the whole system has flipped. Where it was once the boss who would pay to ensure you a comfortable retirement (not to mention bestow upon you that coveted gold watch, or something similar, at the end of 30 or 40 years of service), the onus now falls on you. This is another reason why I strongly urge my clients to keep working in their primary careers for as long as they can. The longer they work, the longer they're putting money away to use during their retirement.

There is another type of pension plan called the defined benefit pension plan. This is specifically designed for a business that has a smaller group of employees. An example of a good fit would be a medical practice or accounting firm. It works very well if the owner makes substantially more income than the other employees and is older. In this type of plan, you can put away well in excess of $100,000 every year. In a traditional pension plan the limit you can put away is significantly less.

I have a client named John who was a commodities broker in the coffee business. He's a very buttoned-up guy – literally. John would even wear a suit and tie to breakfast on Sunday morning! After he retired from the company he worked for, he started his own company with one employee. We put a Defined Benefit Plan in place for him and it yielded nothing but good news. He put away over $125k every year for many years. Instead of netting a half million dollars annually and paying taxes on $450k, he made $500k and paid taxes on only $375k because of the spread he put away in the plan. Definitely a best-case scenario!

John then referred me to a couple, Anthony and Yvonne, who had a landscaping company. We put the same Defined Benefit Pension Plan in place for them as we did for John. The major difference with them was that they started taking money out of their plan in order to create an ATM business. At the end of the day, their plan, which had taken on assets and was ripe to support a healthy retirement for both of them, was reduced to next to nothing because they put it all into that ATM business, which eventually folded. They were left with no business and no money for retirement. In fact, they were broke. This is a crucial point – when you have a pension plan, use it for a pension, not speculative fantasy!

Staying in the Game

There are many non-financial issues specific to retirement that you also need to consider as you approach this stage. For some, bodies – or minds – don't work as well as they used to, which is why they have no choice but to retire. However, I believe that if there is no pressing physical reason to stop working – which there often isn't since most of us aren't working in the coal mines anymore – you should keep on going. Maybe you start working at a lower-stress job, or even, if possible, cut back your hours in your existing position or profession so you can enjoy some family and leisure time. If you can still work and want to, you shouldn't feel pressured to stop working by others, or by yourself; age is just a number, not an imperative.

I think it's a great idea to use your retirement to explore a different field, and potentially start a new career. Not only will it keep you active and mentally sharp – it will also provide a paycheck. While the money may not be anywhere near what you were making in that 40-year career, it's still a cushion. You can still maintain a familiar lifestyle, but simply work fewer or more flexible hours. With this kind of pace change, you may discover that you actually enjoy staying in "the game." I think remaining productive keeps you mentally alert, contributory, and less subject to boredom or depression. We are no longer an agricultural or manufacturing economy: most of us use our minds, not our bodies. Why stop using all our accumulated wisdom just because we've reached a certain milestone birthday?

Baby Boomers and Retirement

Baby Boomers grew to adulthood in the aftermath of the Great Depression. Their parents saw first-hand just how uncertain the economy could be, and how you could go overnight from being solidly middle class to losing everything. Their parents tried to instill in them a strong savers' mentality so that even if the stock market did crash again, or something similarly devastating happened, they would be as prepared as humanly possible.

On the other hand, Baby Boomers also grew up in a prosperous time in American history. A large percentage went to college, and many were able to land white-collar jobs as managers, office workers, and executives upon graduation – not like the seamstresses, factory workers, and electricians, carpenters, and other types of jobs their parents held which required on-the-job vocational training rather than an extended, formal higher education such as college and beyond. This was the first generation whose jobs were based more on their education than on their apprenticeships, so for them, education was mandatory. And, since their parents had been such savers, Boomers were able to rely on parental assistance for a longer period of time. Many even come to expect a substantial inheritance. I don't mean to pick on Baby Boomers, but since I am of this generation, it is a demographic I can examine closely – even if it does require a good deal of self-reflection in the process.

Wants vs. Needs

I think we often get our "wants" confused with our "needs." The older generation didn't have that problem. Credit card companies didn't exist in the same massive way they do now; in any case our parents didn't buy much – if anything – on credit. If they didn't have the money to buy something, they didn't spend it. Instead, they saved up and only spent their money when it became absolutely necessary.

The rise of credit card companies had a profound effect on consumerism. Suddenly any and everything was available with the swipe of a card, and the "buy now, figure out how to pay for it later" mentality developed. I remember sitting with my father in our living room when I was a young child and he was just staring at this little piece of plastic, his first credit card. He couldn't believe that he'd just come from the store, handed the sales clerk this piece of plastic – with no dollars or coins involved!

Now that people were switching from using actual money to buying on credit, people began to lose track of what they were spending. It didn't feel like they were spending money. In a way, it's a more comfortable and tidy transaction. You see something, you want it – you don't necessarily need it – and tell yourself you'll worry about paying it when the bill comes in. Then you don't even want to open the credit card statement.

Consumer culture has people believing that they'd be so much happier by acquiring more things. In reality this dictum that encouraged people to buy more was a result of the "keeping up with the Joneses" mindset, the "you are what you own" mentality, which came to us from advertising and other forms of media. It also perhaps comes from an even more compelling, if misguided, source: the desire of human beings to be liked, respected and admired. Alas, one doesn't really need to go into debt for that.

Whatever the complete cocktail of reasons, it's no wonder that a great many Baby Boomers are not prepared when it comes to retirement – buying on credit has allowed people to think that their funds are bottomless, and now people find themselves ill equipped to manage their finances when faced with the reality of a fixed income.

Staying Inspired

Again, I'll say it: if you age healthfully in mind, body and spirit, there's no real reason you need to retire. In the traditional sense, if you want to retire from your main career after working there for thirty years or so, that is possibly a good idea. But again, I urge my clients to use their extra time wisely. People may be living longer, but we still are not living forever. Use this next stage to try something you've never been able to try before. If you don't want to get another job, maybe try to set up a consultancy where you can put all that accumulated experience and insights to good use. At the same time, why not take that road trip to the Grand Canyon you've always been meaning to take? Above all, I am encouraging you to take part in something that challenges you and helps you continue to learn and grow until your last breath.

Do you want to know what's going on in our country today? Do you want to get a fresh, new perspective and re-energize yourself? Go hang out with kids in their 20s, maybe your own grandkids. That's exciting, and gives you an opportunity to stay young.

"But Paul, what if I don't have any grandchildren?" you might ask. Don't worry – you're not alone. Try to refrain from haranguing your children to get married and procreate. One thing you can say about Millennials is that they don't jump into things hastily. (The Millennial generation refers to people born between 1980 and 2000. Basically, the generation people my age refer to as "kids today.")

If you don't have any grandchildren or nieces and nephews to dote upon, it's okay. We aren't pressuring our kids to have kids so quickly. Most of them are holding off as they start their careers, buy cars, and settle into homes. It's hard for your son or daughter to hear you ask, "When are we going to become grandparents?" when they are still trying to figure out what they want their lives to look like.

You also don't have to be a biological grandparent to mentor young people. There are many community organizations that offer opportunities to hang out with young people. They may not show it at first, but these young people will be impressed at what you bring to the table. At 65, 70, 75, or even 80 years old, you have many years of experience, expertise, enthusiasm, and a wealth of knowledge, information and enrichment to share. Maybe you can mentor young people who are trying to break into the industry from which you just retired. They're going to be fascinated when you describe how you established your career in a world devoid of cell phones and the Internet! You have a valuable perspective they never had. Why not be generous and pass your insights and wisdom along?

As a man, I'm particularly passionate about personally acting as a role model to the younger generation. Many children of divorce grow up without a strong father figure because they wind up spending more time with their mother. There is a lack of male role models for young people, and I think it's up to us, the older generation of men who might have some time on our hands, to become a mentor for these kids, male or female. Instead of only investing in stocks and bonds, try investing in people and the future by giving of your time and experience.

Retirement for the Modern Age

I've seen people put themselves in what I call "full-blown retirement mode." They often find it very hard to climb out of that mindset and get motivated to do any kind of business again. Others will claim they're just going to "retire for a little bit," and then get back to work. Few people fully retire for a few years and then decide they want to go look for a job again.

My client Stacy is a widow. She had raised four daughters, all of whom were married, and she had a few grandchildren. For a long time Stacy had owned a car dealership with her husband; when he died she owned it herself. After a while she decided it was time to retire. However, after six months she became bored and realized that she needed more. She and I sat down and discussed her options. She said she had always been good with people, loved golf, and really enjoyed entertaining. After some research she found an opening to work at a golf course on Long Island, and she jumped at the opportunity. She was hired, and was so enthusiastic about this new venture and did such a great job that she was quickly promoted to Director of Catering at the golf course. Now she is able to supplement her retirement income while doing something she loves and is good at, while still enjoying this next stage in her life.

Of course each client is different. Retiring at 65 and never working again might actually be the answer for you and your spouse, but frankly the only way, or at least the best way, to determine that is if you sit down and talk with a financial advisor. You might have a general sense of when it would be best for you to retire, but a professional will be able to look at your overall financial picture and understand how it corresponds to the lifestyle you will be able to maintain. Once the advisor does that, an ideal plan can be worked out for you and your family.

However, many of these retirement stories with my clients did not turn out as well as I hoped. I have a client, Saul, who is now in his early eighties. He's married with two adult children who he helps out financially. He first came to me in late 2008, during the economic downturn. While many people were hit hard and incurred some sort of loss, Saul lost nearly 80 percent of his entire fortune, before we ever met.

While most people would instinctually start "tightening their belts," Saul did no such thing. During our first meeting, he was describing his situation, and instead of asking how he should downsize, he asked if I could help him find a job! "Paul, I have fifty years of experience in sales – it's how I made my fortune! But I'm not getting any interviews anymore! Why won't anyone hire me?" he asked. I was shocked. Most people his age would have retired years ago, and would be living comfortable, happy lives. His lack of an income also didn't stop him from pampering his children. Every year on their birthdays – to this day – Saul gives them each a check for $15,000. Even when Saul's wife got sick, and his medical bills went through the roof, he refused to change his lifestyle and be less generous to his grown children.

One morning, I came into work and saw that he'd drawn down nearly $100,000 out of his portfolio. I called him into my office for an emergency session. I said, "Saul, why did you take all of this money out? If you keep spending like this, you're going to be destitute in a few years." Can you believe this – he claimed he didn't do it! I said, "Saul, we have the papers to prove it." I guess some people are so stuck in their ways that even hard proof can't convince them otherwise.

The year after his wife succumbed to her cancer, Saul was forced to sell his home and move in with his daughter. Saul is still my client, and he is no less stubborn than the day I met him.

Next Steps

While Millennials may be decades away from their own retirement, they are very much aware of our country's turbulent financial landscape. Many of them were in college or came of age during the job crisis of the 2000s. One thing I always stress with my clients is that it is never too early to start saving for the future. For couples with small children, for example, starting a college fund and adding to it slowly over the years is always a good idea. Of course life is full of surprises, and it is impossible to be prepared for every eventuality. However, working with a knowledgeable professional can help you create a plan for the future starting with where you are now, covering all bases and ensuring a smooth transition to other parts of your life.

Hopefully, I have given you food for thought about your own retirement. In the following chapter, I am going to discuss a different type of planning – estate planning. This is distinct from planning for retirement because it has to do with what comes "after." This is unquestionably a sensitive subject, but one you really do have to address if you want to do the best with your remaining assets for your children and also for yourself. That is, unless you're satisfied to do nothing, and by default leave it all to our common relative – Uncle Sam!

"Sometimes the questions are complicated and the answers are simple"

— *Dr. Seuss*

7

Decisions: Making Sure Your Estate Goals Are Met

One of my main objectives in writing this book is to help you find the right financial partner who can help you prioritize your goals and then help you firstly by creating a balanced portfolio that allows you to live the life you want, in the present and in the future. That process begins when you give serious thought to what you feel is most important. Do you need income from your assets and investments? Do you not need income at the moment and mainly want your portfolio to appreciate? Do you need some income and at the same time want your assets to grow so it replaces all or at least some of what you take out to live on? Also, are you interested in leaving a specific inheritance to your loved ones? Or perhaps you want to start a new business yourself or help your adult kids start a business. You might want to plan for retirement, or use some of your savings to purchase a second home.

Your goals may include several of these wants, simultaneously, or your situation may be entirely different. Whatever your specific intentions, it is crucial for you to decide what you want to achieve, hopefully, as you embark on this journey with a trusted and capable financial advisor. When you have your individual endpoints in mind, it is that much easier for you to work together to take the necessary steps that will get you to where you want and need to go. You must also assess your risk tolerance, meaning the degree of variability in investment returns that you are willing to withstand.

Whatever your main priorities, you first must make sure that your portfolio is well prepared for what I call the "big three" circumstances – if you die too soon, live too long, or get sick along the way. You need to begin there. If your advisor isn't focused on ensuring that from the start, you may, someday in the not too distant future find yourself adrift, or might be leaving your family adrift – as happened in the two cautionary tales I described in Chapter Two.

Keep Calm and Carry On

At some point in your life you will most likely experience some financial insecurity – in truth everyone does. Even the wealthiest among us have moments of uncertainty about money. It is in these uncertain moments that we need to resist pushing the panic button. I too can become emotional when faced with market downturns or other complications, but I've learned how to stay calm, make wise choices, and move forward effectively for my clients. If your financial advisor panics, it's like dropping a match into a pool of flammable liquid – everything goes up in flames!

To me, panicking inhibits taking productive action. When you become paralyzed by fear, you develop tunnel vision and only see the one thing that's stressing you out. For extreme worrywarts, panicking leads to making mistakes and can become a self-fulfilling prophecy. My job is to curb any panic that might arise, and make sure that if things don't go exactly as we expected, there's always a powerful Plan B to fall back on.

It May Be Their Inheritance, But It's Your Money Now

When my clients ask me whether they should be more concerned with leaving an estate or taking care of themselves while they're still alive, I assure them that it's possible to do both. It's all about balance. Many people understandably want to leave something behind for their families. At the same time, we as a population are also living longer. I truly believe we should enjoy our remaining years and live our lives to the fullest extent—which means being generous to ourselves.

Can we really accomplish this dual objective? The answer is yes. Let's be honest here. For example, you can establish a life insurance policy to ensure that no matter what happens to the rest of your estate – even if you live to be 100 and spend it all on yourself – your adult children or other loved ones will receive a specified amount of money that is potentially tax-free. However, keep in mind, if you plan on purchasing a life insurance policy without the help of an advisor, that not every policy is right for everyone. You'll have to get some input to find the one that suits your needs. People of all socioeconomic statuses should have life insurance, so that, even if whatever else you leave behind is modest, you'll still be providing support for your loved ones. In regard to this last part, please remember how my father having overlooked this aspect of his financial planning negatively impacted my mother's life and mine.

Insurance is about managing risk. It's an economic tool. I have heard people say, "I don't believe in insurance." They can be as "life insurance agnostic" as they like and not believe in it, but when they die they are going to leave a mess behind. One of the cool things about life insurance is that if it is set up properly the proceeds can be free of estate taxes and income taxes. This is a huge benefit that cannot be overlooked.

Inheritance, as you can imagine, can cause some conflict and bad feelings among siblings and even create permanent animosity or rifts. I had one client named Josie who came to me about a year after her mother, Karen, passed away. Karen had left Josie and her younger sister, Lauren, a large inheritance to split evenly between them. Both daughters had husbands and children of their own so the money – two million each – would go a long way. However, the sisters reacted quite differently. Lauren immediately took her inheritance and spent a lot of it. She made loan payments, she and her husband bought a new car, they took a family vacation, and many other things. Before they knew it, the inheritance was dwindled. Josie, on the other hand, kept her inheritance locked up tightly and wouldn't touch it for anything.

Josie came to me because she was afraid that Lauren would start asking her for money. "First things first," I said to Josie. "You're not doing your inheritance any favors by letting it sit in your bank account." Josie was shocked. She thought I was going to praise her for being so prudent and join her in reprimanding her sister for being so flippant.

As I explained, "Your sister might have spent a lot of the money already, but she put a good deal towards things that she really needed. She was able to pay off bills, and also spend quality time with her family."

Ultimately, Josie could see where I was coming from, and we wound up working together to establish an intelligent plan for her inheritance. She was still rather tightly wound, but in the end, I was able to help her make her inheritance work for her in the best way possible.

The Fine Line Between Confident and Stubborn

Some of my older clients become somewhat anxious when it comes to spending their savings on themselves. They say, "Paul, I don't want to spend too much of my money now because I want to make sure my children have it when I die." I understand the impulse. You want to make sure your children, grandchildren, and whoever else is important to you are well taken care of after you're gone. Still, to me it's a huge mistake to let this way of thinking diminish your own happiness at a time when you should be celebrating this later stage of life – your own Act Three.

This, however, is a complex issue and one that strikes such a chord in me with regard to my own life. When my father died, my mother received $5,000 from his burial policy. She tried to keep his business running, but all the stress made her sick. She eventually sold the business for $64,000. With that modest amount she had to make her way in the world. She had to compromise her lifestyle at every turn just to provide and to satisfy her desires to leave something for me when she died. That desire upset me because I wanted her to enjoy what she could out of whatever money she had. I didn't want to be the person who was being sacrificed for. I wanted her to go have a juicy steak once in a while instead of eating matzo and cottage cheese for lunch every single day.

But some people are just stuck in their ways and always will be, especially when they're operating with a Depression mentality. Take my clients Randall and Bea. They are 88 and 84 respectively and live in Washington Heights, which is at the northern most end of Manhattan. Their children and grandchildren live further downtown, and on the east side, in Murray Hill. They visit often, usually on Sunday nights for dinner. When it's finally time for them to go home, instead of springing for a taxi, they insist on taking two buses and walking several blocks – even in the pouring rain or snow! Anything they can do to save a buck, they will do. It doesn't matter how much money they have, and they have a good amount – plenty, at least, for a cab ride uptown! Even when they eat out, they are very frugal about it. They go to the diner and get one entrée to share, and then bring home leftovers. They relish the free salad and dessert that comes with the meal, and they even take handfuls of those free cookies the diner has at the register. It's those little things that are very telling and let you know that someone has a depression mentality.

Randall and Bea are just too scared to spend their money because "you never know when disaster might strike." This makes total sense to them. Having clients with this depression mindset definitely makes my job more difficult. One potential client, Simon, came to see me a while back. He was a referral from a longtime client named George. Both men were 93 years old at the time. George, who had grown up in Vienna, was still a practicing CPA. He would question me constantly. "Paul, do you invest your money in new software?" He was testing to see if I was on the cutting edge of technology—which I am. As I was just about to reassure him that I had the latest software, he asked another question: "Do you know the value of my portfolio right now?" In other words, before I can answer one question, he would come out with another one!

On top of everything, though, he always made sure to let me know that he was very satisfied with our relationship. He would say, "Paul, do you know that last year I had the same value as I do today, even though I took out a tremendous amount to live on? Thank you, I am very pleased." "I'm glad you're pleased, George" I told him, "And I appreciate your saying so. It takes a lot of work to make sure that happens." While it was no surprise that he referred me to his friend, Simon, I was still honored to know that he spoke highly of me outside the office. George is an incredible guy for inspiration.

When I spoke with George's friend Simon, I went through the list of his investments that he had emailed to me. That list showed he had about 80 positions, which is a lot for a portfolio. He wanted to know how I felt about each of his assets, so I went through an entire review with him. It took hours. Finally, at the end of several conversations, I expected him to say, "OK, let's move ahead." Instead he said, "Not so fast."

Simon was clearly getting anxious, and had mixed feelings about this situation. He said, "Paul, I want to do better, but I'm nervous – what's going to happen to my money if I die?" I wanted to say, "IF you die?" Remember, the guy was 93 years old! I told him he shouldn't be worried about what could happen – worrying about the inevitable future gets us nowhere. If we get all hung up on the "what ifs" in life none of us would be able to leave the house. Then Simon said, "Well, my son looked at everything, and he thinks he can do a better job managing my own money." I asked Simon if he had ever really tried managing his own money. He said that he hadn't, and that what he had in place now was all due to his son's assessment of what was needed.

"Simon, if your son is such a genius at telling you how to manage your money, why is half of it sitting in a Money Market Fund doing nothing when you are in significant need of additional income." I wanted him to be able to make an informed decision, so I reminded him that it was actually costing him money in fees for it to sit there. He said he understood where I was coming from, but ended the conversation that day without making a commitment to me. He had become reliant on his son managing his account, or at least telling him what to do. He was too stuck in his ways, or perhaps one could say "loyal to a fault," to start changing things – even for the better.

In the end, Simon and his son never became clients of mine. His son actually called to ask if he could hire me on a consulting basis and pay me an hourly rate. I said no. At the end of the day, not every client wants to sign on with me, and even the best intentions and efforts don't always pan out. This story is really not about me: it's about fear, and about listening to relatives as opposed to consulting professionals. The old saying about something you get for nothing is worth nothing truly applies here.

Intelligently Planning for Your Future

Relinquishing some control over your portfolio at some point by working with a professional is something that everyone ideally should come to terms with if they want to do it right. For those clients who have already made arrangements to leave their estates to their spouses and children, relinquishing control might come in a very different way than expected. I have a client named Edmond who, like my buddy Tony, checks in on every share he owns and knows it all off the top of his head. I could almost call him a mathematical genius when it comes to his portfolio. Recently Edmond discovered that his family was planning to throw him a party for his 75th birthday. Not only would this party cost a pretty penny, they were HIS pretty pennies they were going to spend. He said, "Paul, it makes me sick to hear what they want to spend on me. How can I tell them to not do this?"

I could see where he was coming from – he didn't want his funds wasted before he was even gone – but at the same time I feel he could have been more grateful. If he was less stubborn, he could have at least negotiated with his family to throw a somewhat less expensive party.

This party wasn't Edmond's only gripe with his family's projected spending. They had been pushing him to do some estate planning, but Edmond was not into it. In fact, Edmond was so myopic about the whole situation that all he paid attention to were any decreasing numbers on his statements. On the one hand, my thought was, "How could he resent his family for wanting to make intelligent plans for after he's gone to honor his efforts on their behalf?" On the other hand, I did understand how hard he had worked over many decades to secure a comfortable life for his family, and recognized where he was coming from might be the misguided but human reaction of: "Are they already anticipating what they'll get when I die?"

I finally got to talk to Edmond about estate planning – specifically estate liquidity and the importance of it. He didn't want to hear about it. But over lunch his brother showed up because he very much wanted to hear about it. The brothers had the same net worth, just a radically different mindset. His brother said he didn't want 50% of what he owned going to the government when he died. The whole problem, he said, was that his stubborn brother Edmond wanted his assets to show what a big estate he was leaving and did not want to begin making annual gifts. What he didn't realize, his own brother pointed out, was that the bigger his estate was, the more estate tax that would have been paid!

This isn't the first time a client's ego got in the way of making the best choices. He couldn't understand it, but his brother got it all. His brother finally convinced him, allowed me to bring a Trust and Estate attorney into the planning phase, and eventually they both bought a block of life insurance to create liquidity.

I believe that successful investing is all about hands-on management of your money, with attention paid by you to what it's doing for you. It's all about being both proactive and appropriately aggressive with your investments. You want to really make your dollars work for you, not just let your funds sit passively and get reduced bit by bit through the ravages of inflation, little inflationary piranhas. You also want to have some less risky options. To me it's all about balance, along with constant vigilance of the markets and the economy, knowing what each client wants and needs—and knowing that those goals, desires, and situations typically change from year to year.

It's not easy when clients push back against advice I give them that's in their best interest, but I can't let it frustrate me. However, I do have to remind some of my clients that this is what they hired me for – so I can help them look at their assets and accounts intelligently and plan accordingly for whatever the future may bring. As the saying goes, the only constant in life is change!

Honoring Your Parents' Wishes but Forging Your Own Path

I have a client named Danny who brought his mother, Cynthia, into my office. She actually became a client very soon before she died. Danny and Cynthia were a very smart mother and son duo. Both were doctors, and each had their own wishes when it came to their portfolios. I did my best to help them achieve their specific goals. Right after Cynthia died Danny and I had a meeting. He said, "Paul, I know you want me to move the money that's in my mother's pension plan to you, but I haven't decided that I want to do that just yet."

Until then, my work with Danny and his money had gone smoothly. Now however I was sensing ambivalence. I knew that he was mourning his mother and that this was a difficult process for him. I also sensed that his mother's death wasn't the only thing that was the cause of his stress. I asked him flat out, "Danny is anything else bothering you?" He said, "I wasn't going to say anything, but yes, it's my wife. I want to make her the beneficiary of my life insurance policies but I don't know if she's completely trustworthy. I feel like she might be setting me up somehow."

I knew this was going to be a challenge. Not only were we dealing with a grieving son, we were also dealing with some kind of marital issue. I said, "Danny, are you aware that, because it's inherited, you have to take distributions from your mother's IRA now? You will have to decide how you want to go about this. But we can if you like set up a Trust within the context of your Will to apportion assets when you pass away directly to your two children and not to your wife." We had a long meeting in which we weighed the pros and cons, but he left without making a solid commitment.

After he walked out of my office that day I didn't hear from Danny for several weeks. It was not like Danny to not return my calls, and I was worried, so I finally called him. I got his answering machine. I said, "Hi Danny, it's Paul. I'm calling because I'm concerned. Are you okay? Is everything all right? Call me back and let me know." He called back within an hour. "Hey Paul. Listen, I'm really sorry for not responding sooner," he said. "I've been a mess. In terms of my mother's account, I'm leaning towards giving it to you, but I haven't fully made my decision yet." I said, "I understand. Is there anything I can do to help you decide?" He said, "I guess my issue is that my mother has always had her money in this pension plan. I know that I'm now the steward of this money, but it doesn't feel like it's my money. In my head it's still my mother's money, and if this one plan was good for her, I'm thinking it might be good enough for me as well. Can you understand that?"

I thought about it, considering the situation from his vantage point. Ultimately though I had to disagree with him. I said, "Danny, I understand that you're in mourning, but you're going to have to realize – soon – that this is your money. You can leave it there and have different accounts spread across different places, or you can bring it all over here, to people you know and trust and

85

who can and will support you in all aspects of your life. This means you can monitor your money and entrust it with human beings instead of a stranger's voice on the phone. Having said that, I will respect whatever decision you make. But you really do need to decide soon."

When I last checked in, Danny is still thinking…

Many of the stories I related to you in this chapter focused on clients who had to make difficult financial decisions. As you can see, choosing the right person who can help you decide what to do with your assets and also help you take the necessary actions can make a huge difference in the outcome. My goal is to have you learn from these stories so that every decision you need to make, going forward, is a real "make" instead of a "break."

Our next chapter deals with the specifics of choosing a financial professional you can work with. We will examine the overall vetting process that needs to take place so that you can feel comfortable in making that critical decision. I will also provide you with some of the kinds of questions you need to ask of yourself and ask your potential advisor

"The true alchemists do not change lead into gold; they change the world into words."

— *William H. Gass*

8

Alchemy: Ideal Client Meets Ideal Advisor – Let's Get Serious!

Throughout history, in real life and in literature, humans have been obsessed with the possibility of turning nothing much into something of great value. However, what our mothers and fathers always told us is true: money doesn't grow on trees, nor can it be spun from straw like a post-modern Rumpelstiltskin, or grown in a lab – even with the newest "3D printing" technology!

This is also true with regard to finding the perfect professional relationship. Almost all relationships – friendships, romantic relationships, professional partnerships, etc. – take hard work to launch and maintain. Of course it's important that there be an initial "spark," the mutual recognition that you and this advisor have "chemistry" and work well together, but that spark or initial feeling of familiarity is not enough to sustain a partnership of this kind. The biggest factor in creating a relationship of this kind is confidence.

Previously, I've discussed the immense amount of trust that needs to be present in the relationship. What you would need to make this pairing work for both parties, and for the well-being and growth of the project itself: the right kind of asset management that will work for you today, tomorrow, and into the foreseeable future.

The Importance of the First Impression

The first time I was charged with finding clients of my own I was ecstatic; I knew this was the first step in becoming an established finance professional. Quickly following that excitement was also terror. I soon discovered how truly daunting it was going to be to create a clientele. This was where my mentor, Tom Costello, played a huge role by helping me get my footing on the rocky coast that constitutes the financial industry. I learned from his example that the best way to build a clientele was through word-of-mouth and referrals. But of course, as in all industries, that was easier said than done! Especially when it comes to something as important as financial advising, people are more likely to trust someone recommended from a close friend or family member than some anonymous person they found in a phone book or who cold calls them.

Over time, I worked with Tom to create a clear way to explain to potential clients who I was, what my value could be for them, and how I was paid. This last discussion would come at the end of our initial meeting, which was essentially a two-way interview. They were there to see if they wanted to work with me, and I was assessing what their financial and personal needs would be, what kind of clients they would be, and how we could serve them.

Back then my informative talk was pretty lengthy. One of the last things I'd say was: "If you're like most people, you're probably wondering how I get paid. I get paid in two ways. One: if you think the ideas I have suggested make sense and you choose to implement them, I'm going to ask that you implement them with me. Is that fair? Two: If you think you've benefitted from the work we've done together today, I hope that, just as [your friend] referred you, that you too will introduce me to three other people that you think might need our services and might agree to see me because of their relationship with you."

I further explained to this new prospect, who I was already asking for referrals, that I would only reach out to those they recommend by sending a little card introducing myself and ask them to call me if interested or let me know I could call them. If they agreed to talk with me, then I would reach out. I'd tell the original recommended client that some of the friends they referred may or may not become clients, and that this should not concern them at all: that I would just appreciate the introductions.

What I quickly learned was that people don't want to be asked to give referrals, especially so early on in our budding client-advisor relationship. No matter how great a financial advisor you are, the person you are speaking with will understandably tend to have his or her guard up when you talk about recruiting other clients during their meetings. It makes them feel as if their business isn't sufficient enough for you, even if that is not your intent.

Now, after decades of experience, I've perfected my "first impression." I treat each and every meeting with a client – whether new or long term – as a separate entity. I have found that with a little patience and trust on my part, most clients, once they can see what their advisor is doing and has done for them, will eventually refer their friends and family members. But it must be on his or her own timetable. This way of building a business is like farming rather than hunting. You grow the relationship with all the small and large successes, "watering the plants," rather than going out to kill and eat. Over the years, my client base did grow – and is still growing – because of referrals. Much like cultivating a garden, patience goes a long way.

The Dos and Don'ts of Finding an Advisor

During the initial meeting with a prospective financial advisor, you will likely discuss your short- and long-term financial goals in order to give your advisor a good sense of your priorities. Although this is a straightforward process, the meeting will probably be somewhat stressful, especially if you've never before undertaken any kind of revealing financial conversation. It's almost like taking a financial x-ray!

Most financial advisors will be sensitive to this, but it's still important to be up front with them about your experience or lack thereof. On the flip side, if you do have a lot of experience with finances, and what you're looking for now is an advisor to help you with a large purchase or to intelligently revamp your portfolio because of certain life changes (a job or business change, a death, a marriage or divorce, a health crisis or other disaster), it's important to let them know that too. This way you don't have to start from square one and you can jump right into the heart of the matter.

- Have a general idea about the answers to the following questions:
- What are big upcoming events in your life? This includes getting married, having a child, preparing to welcome a grandchild, sending a child or grandchild to college, getting a divorce, and/or retiring.
- What are your financial goals for the short and long term? This includes saving for a house or a vacation home, selling a home and moving, starting a college fund, paying off debt, starting a new business, etc.
- Do you have specific investment pursuits? If not, do you want to? How would you like them to be implemented?
- How much involvement do you want to have in the process? Some clients want to be more hands-on – others trust me to take care of everything. I find the ideal is a balance between the two, but again, it's up to you.
- Be upfront about your current financial situation. You can exaggerate or underestimate all you want, but an advisor will be able to tell where you're huffing, puffing, or bluffing once he

or she looks at your statements.

- Come prepared. You should expect to discuss a wide range of topics. To make the meeting as productive as possible, bring with you the following documents: the last two years of tax returns, a current bank statement, any retirement information such as IRAs, pensions, or annuities, insurance documentation, loan information, copies of wills and trusts, or mortgages, and investment information including your lifestyle expenses such as the cash you spend regularly, as well as any stocks, bonds and other assets such as gold coins, rare stamps, art, and other valuable collectibles, real estate holdings, etc.

- Ask questions. This is your money and your future. If you feel unclear about anything, ask! He or she is there to help you, not discourage you. Do be wary of criticism or negativity. If you feel you're being talked down to, move on!

DON'T

- Expect financial advisors to be god-like. Too many times I hear this said, in these words in essence: "How will you ensure that all my needs are taken care of at all times?" While it would be nice to guarantee that every client's financial needs are always met, it's simply not feasible. Managing a portfolio isn't like building something concrete, and once it's done it's done, you just sit back and enjoy what you've built.

- In finance, laws change and your life changes. Things are always changing, so every need is never permanently taken care of and needs to be watched. In fact, each client's portfolio is a living, breathing, constantly changing entity. Think of this analogy: you have a young kid, and as soon as you find a perfect pair of shoes, his feet seem to grow overnight, and suddenly you need to buy him a new pair. Advisors are not mind readers – the only way we will know how to take care of your financial needs is if you help us keep the lines of communication open and report on any changes in your life and in your wants, needs, and goals, personally and professionally.

- Challenge their fees. Challenging any professional's fees immediately is a sure-fire way to shut down the conversation. It is also off-putting if you mention a competitor who charges less. Instead of putting up a wall, try to listen to what the advisor has to offer you. If you let them explain, you might be pleasantly surprised with what you'll be getting for your fees. I know that I offer a high tech and high touch boutique environment. If that is meaningful to you, then I'm your guy. In my experience, if your only goal is to find the cheapest product or service, the quality you get will reflect that.

- Bad-mouth a previous advisor. It's a huge red flag if a client comes to me with a laundry list of complaints about their last financial advising experience. Think of it as if it were a romantic relationship: It's never a good sign if your significant other constantly bad-mouths his or her exes. It becomes suspicious if every one of their former partners is described as being lazy or crazy. Clearly there's a pattern, and more often than not, at least a good deal of the time, the responsibility falls on the one complaining. Similarly in a professional financial venture, if a client has had a bad experience with every previous advisor, it makes them seem pretty hard to work with, or worse. Plus, imagine what they'll say about you if your partnership sours!

Going With the Flow

As Thomas Edison once said, "Nobody has cornered the market on ideas." Maybe you have a different perspective on your portfolio than your current advisor, or you want to garner a different opinion on how your portfolio should be handled. I always encourage people to meet with and compare the pros and cons of different financial advisors before they make a decision. Remember that this job is to offer you advice, not an end-all be-all edict as to what you ought to, should, or must do with your assets.

People and relationships are constantly changing. I know I said this before, but I have to say it again. Between divorce, illness, accidents, and other events in life's ever-changing panorama, it's impossible to predict with complete accuracy what your life is going to look like in a year, let alone in a day. It's unfortunate when people think things are set in stone, and then one of those unexpected "things" happens.

I had a client who thought this way. He was an older gentleman who was very stuck in his ways. He had a solid ten-year financial plan that he wouldn't budge on. Try as I might to convince him to be more flexible in his outlook he remained headstrong. Unfortunately, his entire plan was turned on its head when his wife was diagnosed with Alzheimer's Disease. At that juncture, their whole lives, personal and financial, were drastically changed, and the client was forced to rethink his entire plan. For one thing, we were left scrambling to find money for her medical bills. Sadly, within a year we also had to make funeral arrangements. We had to transfer funds from various accounts at the last minute, creating more stress on an already tragic situation. This is why there are financial advisors—to make sure that this kind of last minute scrambling does not happen. This is one of the main reasons why I'm around.

From My Side of the Table

While many financial professionals will want to "court" you, they can only offer so much advice and so much of their time before you're "on the clock." I can't tell you how many times I've found myself in a social setting where people have just found out that I'm a money manager. Some people will actually corner me to ask a ton of questions about their portfolio or some decision they have to make right now – all while I'm standing there holding a plate of hors d'oeuvres in one hand and a drink in the other!

While I'm always happy to help, and honored that near-strangers are seeking my advice, this is my business, my trade, and my expertise. A baker can only give away so many free slices and samples before he has to charge for a whole cake! I'm sure many of you can empathize—especially if you're a doctor or dentist who gets cornered at a party for an instant diagnosis.

A Two-Way Street

Of course I try to be objective and non-judgmental when it comes to business, but being human, there are certain types of people I enjoy working with more than others. As I've said, when I'm working with you and your family, I'm with you 100%. So when I'm considering taking on a new client, it has to be someone I enjoy spending time with. I love working with people who have a sense of humor, people who can take direction, and people who aren't looking to impress me with their knowledge, especially when it's clear they still have a lot to learn. A healthy interest in music doesn't hurt either—remember my roots and passion for music.

I value my clients and am constantly learning from their personal stories. The people I enjoy being around the most, both in my personal life and in my business, are people who can celebrate other peoples' successes, not just their own. They can appreciate other's achievements. They want to see me and my other clients do well, and feel empowered by others people's accomplishments. They

96

aren't overly competitive, and they don't let jealousy get the best of them. They realize that just because someone else did better in one quarter, this doesn't necessarily say anything negative about them, or their advisor. It just means they have a different portfolio with different needs.

My ideal clients are not the type of people who will say, "My friend's financial advisor got them X amount of dollars in return – why can't you get this for me?" First of all, what did your friend's portfolio look like? Is it anywhere close to yours? What are their assets? More often than not, competitive clients like this try to blame their own financial shortcomings on their advisor. I can only work with what you've brought to me. I can't pretend that you have more money than you do. A major part of my job is helping my clients come to terms with their financial realities, whatever those may be.

I had a wealthy client who would always compare his investments with me to his investments with other people, and one in particular: Bernie Madoff. That's correct! This was before the scandal broke. One day I was out to lunch with this client and a few of his friends. The entire lunch he bragged to them about how much appreciation I'd gotten him on his investments. He was trying to impress his friends. When I looked around the table at them, I saw that they were looking at each other, mortified. They didn't care how much he had and were embarrassed for him. It was inappropriate to let people know his net worth. This is a major "don't" – don't tell people how much money you have. Nobody cares and it's confidential. Plus, this guy had actually compared me to Madoff! He had money with Madoff too, and would always say how much Madoff was working for him. Well, we all know the end of that story!

I am really interested in my clients' stories and learning where their true passions lie. One of my very successful clients works out on Long Island in the pharmaceutical industry and has a passion for space exploration. Then there's a straight-laced guy named Vincent who, as it turns out, is an avid motorcycle enthusiast! He rides a Harley every weekend when the weather allows. That is what moves me – the human dynamic and people's unexpected interests.

My client Harry, who I described in an earlier chapter, calls the office often and I always feel better after having chatted with him, even if it has nothing to do with his portfolio, or even finance in general. He's the type of guy who can appreciate the little things. He will sometimes call me up just to tell me he heard a song that reminded him of me, or to tell me a funny story.

Surprise, Surprise

I've learned a lot from my time as a financial professional, and am still learning. I believe this gives me an advantage. In addition to our firm, Capital Estate Advisors, Inc., being a Registered Investment Advisor, I'm also a Licensed Insurance Broker and a Certified Financial Planner. Certified, licensed, and registered. Some might say I'm a "triple threat." However I never let my years of experience get in the way of learning something new. I've had clients from all walks of life, but the minute I start thinking, "I've seen it all" I get a completely new client who surprises me.

Some surprises are welcome and some are not so welcome. I'll offer an example of a pleasant surprise first. I was referred to a guy named Jack. He was married with four kids and made his fortune by buying, developing and owning prime commercial real estate around New York City. I began by talking with him about estate planning and the devastating effects taxes would have on his now mostly illiquid assets. I was trying to get him to understand the impact of estate taxes after he and his wife died, and what his children would really be left with. You have heard me discuss this before!

I really pulled out all the stops for him because I thought I could be of great service to him and that he would be a perfect fit for my company. I took him to the New York Athletic Club for lunch and even asked an associate of mine, one of the top Trust and Estate attorneys in NYC, to join us. But, despite my best efforts, Jack refused to move ahead. I asked him to reconsider, but he wouldn't budge. Needless to say, I was disappointed because I'd put in a good deal of time and effort, and thought we were a match.

A year later, after I had all but forgotten about Jack, I got a phone call from him. After some pleasantries he said, "Paul, listen, I know I was difficult last year. After much discussion with my wife, we realized we were spending too much time focusing on estate planning. We decided that we're not all that concerned, not yet anyway, about what will happen after we die. I'd rather concentrate on what we have while we're still alive. If you're still up for it, I'd like to work with you and engage you to manage our money."

Of course I said yes. I was surprised and delighted that he had taken the time to redefine his goals. Once he and his wife agreed on a plan, they were able to proceed with my help. The day after that phone call, he dropped off the documents and transferred his investment assets from a different firm into his new account with us.

Unfortunately not all surprises from clients are this positive. I was referred to a client named Christopher, who owned a very successful construction company in New York. He and his wife were both 75 years old. I ended up getting them two significant life insurance policies that would pay all taxes on their estate after their demise. The combined premium for these new insurance policies on both of them was about $100,000 a year. They cut checks for about $50,000, half of it. They paid the other half out of an old life insurance policy they already had, which had a significant cash value. With my guidance, Christopher elected to receive income from that life insurance policy by having the cash value transferred to an annuity. The plan was for the annuity to pay him income for a period of ten years. He was going to get an annual check for $50k for ten years from the annuity, and would use that to pay the other half of the new premium.

This all seemed to be working smoothly for the next couple of years. Then one day I got a call from his insurance carrier for the old policy. They told me they needed to talk to me about Christopher. They said that Christopher and his wife were supposed to be getting $50k a year from this annuity—which I knew— but that they, the insurance company, had made an error and had been mistakenly paying them $50k each month! At that point this had been happening for about six months.

I was shocked. I called Christopher immediately and asked if they knew about it. Without hesitation he and his wife both said yes, they knew they'd gotten that money. I said, "Why didn't you tell me this was happening?" Christopher said, "Well, I figured they'd catch up sooner or later." Over those six months he had accrued $300,000, which went into his pocket through an accounting error. Instead of reporting the error he kept quiet about it. Obviously the company did "catch up" with it. And of course, as I told Christopher would happen, they wanted all of that money back.

To my further shock and chagrin Christopher said, matter-of-factly, "I'm not giving it back. It was their screw-up." I couldn't believe what I was hearing and actually had to explain to this man that that's not how it works. I had no idea his ethics were so bad. That was a rare event, but one dramatic example of a way a client surprised me that was certainly not a good way. Interestingly, immediately after this debacle, this couple cashed out of the new policies they had gotten through me. In other words, they wound up terminating themselves as clients right before I could do so.

Keeping an Open Mind

I believe every client is unique, and that's how I treat them. Even if a new client's situation seems almost identical to one I've dealt with in the past, I approach each new person and his or her situation with an open mind. Avoiding preconceived notions is difficult but necessary. I am always hopeful that this open-minded and openhearted attitude is reciprocal. You'll never get anywhere with your portfolio – or get the best from your financial advisor – if you come at this with a stubborn or rigid attitude.

Being open-minded will definitely help you when you're looking for the right financial professional. Perhaps you've had some challenging experiences with one or more finance professionals in the past. Things happened that were not as positive as you'd hoped for. Again I want to emphasize that there is nothing wrong in being guarded, asking questions, and listening carefully to the answers to see if you share good chemistry and a similar philosophy. However, if you walk into an advisor's office with a chip on your shoulder you are likely sabotaging a potentially rewarding relationship before it even begins.

Many twists and turns occur in our lives, and in the lives of those we love. Making sure your money is safe, growing, and supports you for as long as you need requires a lot of attention to detail on the part of both the client and advisor. This is not something to be taken lightly. Still, the fact is that most people spend more time deciding what restaurant to go to and what to eat for dinner than they do attending to their financial affairs. I don't want that to be your situation. Even multi-millionaires and billionaires work hard for their money. I have too much respect for my clients— and for the power of a well-balanced portfolio – to ever let that happen.

For those who might want to corner me for my next round of advice, I will give it freely. Just do me a favor: please don't do it when I have a plate of hors d'oeuvres in one hand and a drink in the other. Call my office!

In the next chapter we're going to get into some nitty-gritty details and descriptions from the world of money management. I want to give you a few specifics that can help you understand the concepts behind the jargon.

"Money is only a tool. It will take you wherever you wish, but it will not replace you as the driver."

— *Ayn Rand*

9

Snapshots: Definitions to Help You Navigate and Communicate

By this point in the book, you may have run into unfamiliar terms such as "bond funds," "annuities," "IRAs" and "the Dow." So you can feel more confident in your growing financial knowledge, I will go through some of the most important terms and definitions.

What Exactly is a Financial Advisor?

In its most basic terms, a financial advisor meets with clients and counsels them on their finances. This could mean sitting down and creating budgets for their everyday lives, establishing retirement plans, or advising them on their investments. While it's not in the typical job description, advisors can also invest a client's funds and meet with them on a regular basis to discuss these investments.

I've shared many stories with you on my interesting, surprising, challenging, and often downright exciting clients. My job requires me to establish a safe, comfortable future for all of them. A good part of my job is all about maintenance. However, as you have seen in the stories I've shared, financial advisors are also there to be keeping assets steadily working for the client. This is especially important when the unexpected occurs. We are there to support our clients during their financial troubles – we help them make sense of their situation and together we establish a solid plan for moving forward. It's not about simply doing the work for my clients; it's about tackling their financial goals as a united force.

The Professions: CLU vs. CFP® vs. Money Managers

There are many other professions in the financial industry that do a relatively similar job, but the certification processes are different and they each have their own specialty. You've likely heard of them by their acronyms: CLU, CFP®, CFA. I'll try to be as clear as I can and differentiate them for you.

The Chartered Life Underwriter (CLU) designation is one of the oldest and most respected credentials in financial services, dating back to the late 1920s. Their areas of specialty are advanced life insurance and estate planning.

A Certified Financial Advisor (CFP®) is one of the top generalist qualifiers a financial advisor can achieve. This means the individual has passed a rigorous program that covers a broad base of financial planning subject areas and can train certificants in the discipline of financial planning. CFP® certification candidates must have attained a Bachelor's Degree and must have completed at least three years of full-time financial planning-related experience. CFP® candidates must also pass all course exams and, upon completion of the educational requirements, must sit for the national CFP® Board exam.

A Chartered Financial Analyst (CFA) is respected for providing real-world knowledge for working investment professionals. For almost 50 years the CFA mark has represented rigorous in-depth education for top investment analysts. The CFA exams are widely considered to be extremely difficult, with pass rates sometimes below 50% for each of the three levels. The education in this arena covers a broad range of topics relating to investment management, financial analysis, stocks, bonds and derivatives, and also provides a generalized knowledge of other areas of finance.

A Money Manager is a specialized type of financial advisor. They help clients look after their investments and can suggest ways in which to grow the investments, so that clients can reach their financial goals. If a client doesn't really know what their goals are and haven't thought about where they'd like to be financially in the future, the money manager will offer to sit down and counsel them in order to help them define realistic goals.

What is a Portfolio?

I've tossed the word "portfolio" around quite a bit, but for those of you who are unsure as to what this term encompasses, it basically just means a collection of investments held by an investment company, hedge fund, financial institution or individual. A lot of people will ask me what the "perfect" portfolio looks like. Just as how it would be next to impossible to describe a perfect person, there's definitely no one perfect portfolio because these are so tied to the individual. In a perfect world, a perfect portfolio would have 100% of your assets guaranteed to never depreciate, 100% of your assets generating a return of 10% or more all with growth opportunity on the upside. If you find it, let me know, because it doesn't exist. Also, keep in mind that every portfolio, even some of my wealthiest clients' portfolios, needs constant upkeep.

What is ideal is what is going to be ideal in the moment for you, and even that is subject to change as your life changes. If you want a guarantee of never losing your principal, be aware you're never going to get the higher rates of interest on your money. You also need to know that there's a risk/reward tradeoff. All of these things come with tradeoffs, and this is part of what we discuss: your risk tolerance and what you might be willing to put at some risk for a potentially greater reward.

The Dow Jones

The Dow Jones Industrial Average (DJIA), more commonly

referred to as "the Dow," is one of the oldest and most watched indexes in the world. Including companies like General Electric, Disney, Microsoft, and Exxon, it is a price-weighted average of 30 significant stocks traded on the New York Stock Exchange and the NASDAQ. When TV networks or other news outlets say, "The market is up today," they are generally referring to the Dow. The Dow Jones was at one time the most renowned index for U.S. stocks, but because it only contains 30 companies, most people believe that S&P is a better representation of the U.S. market.

The S&P 500

Standard & Poor's (S&P) is an index of 500 stocks chosen for market size, liquidity, and industry grouping, among other factors. It is designed to be a leading indicator of U.S. equities and is meant to reflect the risk/return characteristics of the large cap universe. Companies included in the index are selected by the S&P Index Committee, a team of analysts and economists at Standard & Poor's. It is one of the most commonly used benchmarks for the overall U.S. stock market.

Mutual Funds

A Mutual Fund is a company that pools money from many investors and invests the money in securities such as stocks, bonds, and short-term debt. Investors buy shares in mutual funds and each share represents an investor's part ownership in the fund and the income it generates. Mutual funds are a popular choice among investors because they generally offer professional management – the fund managers do the research for you and select the securities and monitor the "performance and diversification". Mutual funds typically invest in a range of companies and industries, which helps to lower your risk if one company fails. Most mutual funds set a relatively low dollar amount for initial investment and subsequent purchases and liquidity. Also, mutual fund investors can easily redeem their shares at any time for the current net asset value (NAV). They may have to pay any redemption fees.

Exchange-Traded Funds (ETF)

An ETF, or exchange-traded fund, is a marketable security that tracks an index, a commodity, bonds, or a basket of assets like an index fund. Unlike mutual funds, an ETF trades like a common stock on a stock exchange. ETFs experience price changes throughout the day as they are bought and sold. ETFs typically have higher daily liquidity and lower fees than mutual fund shares, making them an attractive alternative for individual investors. Because it trades like a stock, an ETF does not have its net asset value (NAV) calculated once at the end of every day like a mutual fund does.

Bond Funds vs. Money Market Funds

Bond Funds and Money Market Funds represent debt obligations of corporations, governmental entities, or city agencies.

Most mutual funds fall into one of four main categories: money market funds, bond funds, stock funds, and target date funds. Each type has different features, risks, and rewards. For our purposes, I want to focus on bond funds and money market funds. Money market funds have relatively low risks. By law they can only invest in certain high-quality, short-term investments issued by U.S. corporations, and Federal, State and local governments. Bond funds have higher risks than money market funds because they typically aim to produce higher returns. Because there are many different types of bonds, the risks and rewards of bond funds can vary dramatically.

Annuities

Annuities ("annuals") are a fixed sum of money paid to the holder each year, typically for the rest of his or her life. Annuities can be used to help you increase your savings, protect what you've saved, or generate a stream of income. Deferred annuities can be a good way to boost your retirement savings once you've made the maximum allowable contributions to your 401(k) or IRA. Like any tax-deferred investment, earnings compound over time, providing growth opportunities that taxable accounts lack.

Deferred annuities have no IRS contribution limits, so you can invest as much as you want for retirement. You can also use your savings to create a guaranteed stream of income for retirement. Depending on how annuities are funded, they may not have required minimum distributions (RMDs). RMDs are the minimum amount you must withdraw from your account each year. The RMD for any year is the account balance as of the end of the immediately preceding calendar year divided by a distribution period from the IRS's "Uniform Lifetime Table." A separate table is used if the sole beneficiary is the owner's spouse who is ten or more years younger than the owner.

Bear in mind that withdrawals of taxable amounts from an annuity are subject to ordinary income tax, and, if taken before age 59, may be subject to a 10% IRS penalty. Some annuities also come with annual charges not found in mutual funds, which will affect your returns.

Deferred variable annuities have funds that have the potential for investment growth. However, this can include types of market risk and could result in losses if the value of the underlying investments falls. Variable annuities are usually appropriate for those with longer time horizons, or those who are better able to handle market fluctuations. Some variable annuities allow you to protect your investment against loss while still participating in potential market growth. Deferred fixed annuities offer a guaranteed rate of return for a number of years. Fixed annuities may be more suitable for conservative investors or for those interested in protecting assets from market volatility. In this way, they're similar to certificates of deposit (CDs).

REIT

A REIT, or Real Estate Investment Trust, is a company that owns or finances income-producing real estate. Modeled after mutual funds, REITs provide investors of all types with regular income streams, diversification, and long-term capital appreciation. REITs typically pay out all of their taxable income as dividends to their shareholders. In turn, shareholders pay the income taxes on those dividends.

Commodities

Commodities are objects that come out of the earth such as oranges, wheat, cattle, gold and oil. People buy and sell commodities based on speculation. For instance, if you thought hurricanes over Latin America were going to destroy much of the coffee crop, you would call your commodity broker and have them purchase as much coffee as possible. If you were correct, the price of coffee would be driven up drastically because the crop had been destroyed by weather, making the surviving harvest worth more. Almost all commodity speculators trade on margin, which results in substantial risk to the invested principal. The odds are heavily against anyone hoping to build permanent wealth in the commodity markets.

401K

A 401(k) is a retirement savings plan sponsored by an employer. It lets workers save and invest a piece of their paycheck before taxes are taken out. Taxes aren't paid until the money is withdrawn from the account. Named for the section of the tax code that governs them, 401(k) plans, arose during the 1980s as a supplement to pensions. But as the cost of running pensions escalated, employers started replacing them with 401(k)s.

With a 401(k), you control how your money is invested. Most plans offer a spread of mutual funds composed of stocks, bonds, and money market investments. The most popular option tends to be target-date funds, a combination of stocks and bonds that gradually become more conservative as you reach retirement.

Like most retirement plans, 401(k) plans have restrictions and caveats. In most cases, you can't tap into your employer's contributions immediately. Vesting is the amount of time you must work for your company before gaining access to its payments to your 401(k). (Your payments, on the other hand, vest immediately.) It's an insurance against employees leaving early. On top of that, there are complex rules about when you can withdraw your money and costly penalties for pulling funds out before retirement age.

IRA

An Individual Retirement Account (IRA) is a retirement plan that allows an individual to save for retirement with tax-free growth or on a tax-deferred basis. There are three main types of IRAs—Traditional, Roth, and Rollover— and each come with its own advantages.

In a **Traditional IRA,** you make contributions with money you may be able to deduct on your tax return and any earnings can potentially grow tax-deferred until you withdraw them in retirement. Many retirees also find themselves in a lower tax bracket than they were in pre-retirement, so the tax-deferral means the money may be taxed at a lower rate. With a **Roth IRA**, you make contributions with money you've already paid taxes on (after-tax) and your money may potentially grow tax-free, with tax-free withdrawals in retirement, provided that certain conditions are met. A **Rollover IRA** is a Traditional IRA intended for money "rolled over" from a qualified retirement plan. Rollovers involve moving eligible assets from an employer-sponsored plan, such as a 401(k) or 403(b), into an IRA.

CDs

Certificates of Deposit (CDs) are common savings products offered by banks and credit unions. The key difference between a regular savings account and a CD is that early withdrawal from a CD in advance of pre-specified term leads to penalty fees. CDs are typically offered in terms of 3 months, 6 months, 1 year, 2 years, 3 years, 5 years or greater, although some exceptions do exist. In exchange for locking away a consumer's cash, CDs usually offer higher yields than a regular savings account. The rates typically increase with the length of deposit terms. Deposits in a bank CD are federally insured by the FDIC for up to $250,000 per depositor, per insured bank. For members of a federally insured credit union, CDs are insured up to the same amount through the NCUA.

Insurance

People can insure just about anything if they want to, but for our purposes, let's focus on life insurance. A life insurance policy is a contract with an insurance company. In exchange for payments, known as premiums, the insurance company provides a lump-sum payment, known as a death benefit, to the beneficiaries in the event of the insured's death. Life insurance is not one-size-fits-all, and should be chosen with your unique needs and goals in mind.

Term life insurance provides protection for a set period of time, such as 10 or 20 years. Typically, premiums remain the same for that time. Term life insurance is generally a less costly option than permanent life insurance. **Whole, or permanent, insurance** is designed to provide lifetime coverage. Because of the lifetime coverage period, whole life usually has higher premiums. **Universal life insurance** is another type of permanent life insurance designed to provide lifetime coverage. Unlike whole life insurance, universal policies are flexible and may allow you to raise or lower your premium or coverage amounts throughout your lifetime. Like whole life insurance, universal life also has a tax-deferred savings component, which may build wealth over time.

Here's an example of how life insurance can work. Let's assume that your wills and trusts have been properly drafted. And let's say that you and your spouse have a combined estate of $25 million. After both of you have passed on, the Federal Estate tax is due within 9 months of death. It would currently be about $6 million.

Where does the money come from? Liquidating assets most likely is the course of action, or having your estate borrow the funds. Liquidation often means loss especially in terms of more taxes or market loss. Plus, keep in mind, even if a loan can be arranged there are still interest charges plus the original $6 million to repay.

The government says the first $11 million comes off the top, free of Federal estate taxes when you and your spouse pass on. On the remaining $14 million, the government wants approximately half within nine months of death. Where does that come from? Selling buildings, cashing in stocks, and whatever else is liquid. The other option is you can give an insurance company 1-

2% of that $6 million each year. That's $60,000 to $120,000 a year. You pay your premium, and when you are gone, the government will get their $6 million from the insurance company. That is called "creating dollars at a discount."

Long-term care insurance is another type of insurance many of my clients have. Unlike traditional health insurance, long-term care insurance is designed to cover long-term services and support, including personal and custodial care in a variety of settings such as your home, a community organization, or other facility.

Long-term care insurance policies reimburse policyholders a daily amount (up to a pre-selected limit) for services to assist them with activities of daily living such as bathing, dressing, or eating. You can select a range of care options and benefits that allow you to get the services you need, when you need them. This is a good option for people who have elderly parents who need advanced assistance, like a round-the-clock, at-home nurse, or people who have severely mentally disabled children who will not be able to provide for themselves, or even live on their own. This type of insurance makes sure the funds are there when they are needed, so that people do not go into extreme debt trying to cover these costs out-of-pocket at the last minute.

Trusts

A trust is essentially a type of fiduciary relationship in which one party, known as a grantor, gives another party, the trust, the right to hold title to property or assets for the benefit of a third party, the beneficiary.

There are two types of trusts. The first is called a **Living Trust**, which goes into effect during the grantor's lifetime. The second is called a **Testamentary Trust**, which is created through the will of a deceased person. Trusts can be revocable or irrevocable. A revocable trust, also known as a "living trust," can help you manage your assets or protect you should you become ill, disabled or simply challenged by the symptoms of aging. Most living trusts are written to permit you to revoke or amend them whenever you wish to do so. These trusts do not help you avoid estate tax because your power to revoke or amend them causes them to continue to be includable in your estate. Irrevocable trusts can't be modified or terminated without the permission of the trustee. The grantor, having transferred assets into the trust, effectively removes all of his or her rights of ownership to the assets and the trust. With irrevocable trusts, assets owned are excludable from the estate of the grantor, and as such provide a tax shelter.

One might choose to create a trust if a beneficiary is under age or has a disability that might impair the person's ability to maintain his or her own finances. This would come in handy for an elderly person wishing to make a very young grandchild a beneficiary, or if someone wants to leave money to someone with a mental disability.

Closed-end fund: A Closed-end Fund is a collective investment model based on issuing a fixed number of shares that are not redeemable from the fund. Unlike open-end funds, managers do not create new shares/units in a closed-end fund. Instead, the shares can be purchased (and sold) only in the market. This is the original design of the mutual fund that predates open-end mutual funds but offers the same actively managed pooled investments. Closed-end funds sold publicly must be registered under both the Securities Act of 1933 and the Investment Company Act of 1940.

Closed-end funds are usually listed on a recognized stock exchange and can be bought and sold on that exchange. The price per share is determined by the market and is usually different from the underlying value or net asset value (NAV) per share of the investments held by the fund. The price is said to be at a discount or premium to the NAV when it is below or above the NAV, respectively.

403(b) Tax Sheltered Annuities: A qualified retirement plan for eligible employees of public schools, tax-exempt organizations and eligible ministers and clergy. This is similar to a 401(k) plan, but mainly for non-profit organizations.

Amortization: Paying off debt in regular payments over a period of time.

Asset: Any resource that has economic value that an individual or corporation owns. Assets are resources that produce cash flow or bring added benefit to the individual or company.

Bear Market: A market condition where securities are falling and investors have a pessimistic outlook on the market as a whole. A downturn of 20% or more for more than two months within multiple indexes like the Dow Jones Industrial Average or the S&P 500 is considered the start of a bear market.

Bond: A debt instrument used by corporations, governments (including Federal, State and City) and many other institutions that are used to generate capital. The investor does not become part owner like a shareholder, but does have a greater claim on the issuer's income than a shareholder.

Bull Market: Opposite of bear market; a market condition where securities rise faster than historic averages, usually from an economic recovery, boom or spike in investor confidence.

Capital Gain: A capital gain is realized when an investment's selling price exceeds its purchase price.

Cash Flow: One of the main indications of a company's overall financial health. Calculated by subtracting cash payments from cash receipts over a period of time (month, quarter, year).

Compound Interest: Interest that is calculated not just on the initial principal but also on the accumulated interest from previous periods. As interest is added back to the principal, the rate of return applies to the entire balance, making the balance grow even faster than simple interest. Simple interest is when the interest is applied only to the initial principal, not the accumulated interest as well.

Credit Report: A summary of a person's credit history, showing historical information such as bankruptcies, loans, late payments, and recent inquiries. Individuals can obtain one free credit report from each of the three credit bureaus each year.

Credit Score: A measure of credit risk that is based on activities such as credit use and late payments. Credit scores can be obtained for a fee from one of the three credit bureaus. One of the most common credit scores in the U.S. is the FICO score.

Debt: An amount owed to a person or corporation for funds borrowed.

Diversification: Spreading risk by investing in a range of investment tools such as securities, commodities, real estate, CDs, etc.

Inflation: The gradual increase or rise in the price of goods over a period of time.

Interest: The fee paid for using other people's money. For the borrower, it is the cost of using other people's money. For the lender, it is the income from renting the money.

Liability: An obligation to repay debt.

Liquidity: The ability of an asset to be converted to cash quickly without sacrificing value or giving a discount on the price.

Net worth: Basic calculation of assets minus liabilities. Used both for corporations and individuals to measure financial health.

Option: A contract that gives the buyer the right, but not the obligation, to buy or sell a security at a price that has been set during a set period of time or certain date.

Prime Rate: The prime rate is the best rate available to a bank's most credit-worthy customer. This is determined by the federal funds rate, the overnight rate at which banks lend to one another.
 Principal: The original investment on which interest is generally paid.

Recession: An economic condition defined by a decline in GDP for two or more consecutive quarters. During a recession, the stock market usually drops, unemployment increases, and the housing market declines.

Risk Averse: An investors desire to avoid risk; a more conservative approach to investing is generally upheld by risk averse investors.

Required Minimum Distribution (RMD): The minimum annual amount required for retirement account holders to withdraw, starting at age 70½. This amount is calculated based on the account value on December 31 of the prior year divided by the factor on the IRS RMD table. RMD does not apply for Roth IRAs.

Share: One unit of ownership in a corporation, security, or limited partnership.

Stock: A proportional share of ownership of a corporation. A company may offer 100 shares of stock and if you own 10, you have 10% ownership of the company.

Tax-deferred: Postponing taxes until a later date. Common tax-deferred vehicles include IRAs, 401(k), Keogh Plans, 403(b), and pension plans.

Yield: The annual rate of return for an investment expressed as a percentage.

"Be clear and be real. Listen carefully. Don't be the smartest person in the room. Do what you do best. Pass the baton."

— *Paul S. Reback*

10

Lifestyle: Making Sure Your Money is Always There to Serve You

The word "lifestyle" conjures up many images. Perhaps you envision palm trees moving gently in the southern California breeze, or your thoughts go to a fast-paced urban environment such as New York City. Maybe it's neither of those but something entirely different, where you immediately picture a yacht and private jet even if you're not the proud owner of any of those. Clearly the term "lifestyle" can mean different things to each of us. For our purposes, though, I am referring to how people choose to live their lives, specifically with regards to their means.

Some people are able to live extravagant lives and still stay well within their means, spending the money they have and not going into debt. Others try to live frugally yet can barely make ends meet or dig themselves out of debt. Most of my clients' lifestyles fall between these two extremes. They have a certain accumulation of wealth, and can generally live comfortable lives, but they also have costly overheads. Most have mortgages, loans, and credit cards payments to keep up with. These monthly and yearly outlays keep them within the boundaries of a certain kind of lifestyle.

Some clients tell me they always dream about taking their family on a luxurious vacation in Europe, or want to buy a condo in the city, or a vacation home in the Hamptons, but their lifestyles prevent them from doing these things. Some are the same way when it comes to investing: they'd rather feel secure in knowing that their

123

money is in the bank for when they need it. This is particularly true for clients who have recently come out of debt. They have finally gotten their heads above water, so they don't want to risk it anymore.

As someone who has seen the gains that people have made by investing intelligently, it is frustrating for me when my clients don't want to address investment risk, but I understand where they are coming from. This is a whole lot better than the clients who have been living beyond their means for way too long, with unfortunate delusions about their financial reality, and come to me with a mountain of debt. These are the clients with the enormous homes, the boats, and the flashy cars and it's pretty much all on their credit cards. The old adages are true: Cash is king, and money doesn't buy happiness. After a while, these clients realize that their lifestyles are excessive and that perhaps it wouldn't be such a bad thing to have two cars instead of four, or one home instead of two, and that there is no shame in wearing last season's wardrobe if it means staying out of debt!

Deciding When and How to Change

As your family grows and changes, your lifestyle will of course also change. Change is inevitable. Think back to events in your life: graduation, marriage, the birth of a child. As your child grew, your needs were vastly different as your child or children entered high school. Perhaps you've gone through a divorce or a death recently. Each one of these life events – marriage, children, divorce, and death – necessitates some sort of lifestyle adjustment. When you get married, there's the requisite merging of assets; when you have children, your budget is directed more towards them and saving for their future, as well as your own retirement. Changes may be precipitated when you or your spouse get a more lucrative position or a big promotion, or sell a business. Your lifestyle can change drastically. No matter what, if you're not careful with your money, it might not serve you as well as it could and should.

For my clients with considerable debt, I explain that they can either perpetuate this self-destructive cycle, or choose to change the way they live. Many people engage in magical thinking. They hope their debt will just disappear if they ignore it. Intuitively, they know better, but it becomes overwhelming so they let it fester. It takes a conscious decision to change your lifestyle, especially later in life.

The vast majority of my clients come to me at a crossroads in their lives. Many are "empty nesters" with grown children either in college or married with their own families. Those clients that have amassed a good deal of disposable assets and perhaps more time – some of them are retired, or soon-to-be retired – are ready to do the things they've always wanted to do. Others, whose funds are suddenly more limited due to ending a career, closing a business, medical expenses, etc. may have to downsize, with downsizing encompassing a lot more than just moving into a smaller home or apartment. That life change requires an entire shift in mindset and relationship to money in the first place. This is where a financial advisor can really come in handy.

In Chapter 6 we discussed retirement, and how downsizing can be an opportunity for you to re-examine your funds and determine exactly how much you need and will continue to need to live comfortably. Again, it comes down to choices. One couple I worked with realized that they would no longer be able to afford their big suburban house on Long Island when they retired. While they loved the area and cherished the sprawling home where they had raised their children, they also realized that maintenance costs to keep up the yard, their pool, the taxes, along with many other hidden costs inside the house, would limit their mobility and keep them in debt. Their family was "grown and had flown." They realized they could make do with less space and still live comfortably, so they moved into an apartment in Manhattan. This was not an easy transition. It was actually quite daunting and required complete focus and a big time commitment. Suddenly, they found themselves discussing new concepts like "storage" and "donation bins."

Clutter is the Enemy

If you want to understand just how much stuff you've accumulated, homeowners and renters alike, decide to move. No matter how many years you've lived somewhere, things will get packed into nooks and crannies you forgot even existed. Once the time comes to move and you're ready to clean out every closet, every drawer, and every crawl space, you realize just how much "stuff" you've saved over the years. This is the same stuff you swore you'd use again or that you were keeping for "sentimental value," such as old baby clothes and children's books, sports equipment, and broken gadgets that you swore you'd fix "someday." Ultimately, people forget what has been hiding in their closets for years. My rule is: if you haven't thought about it in five years – toss it.

In Samuel Taylor Coleridge's The Ancient Mariner, the mariner's constant refrain is "Water, water everywhere and not a drop to drink." In the clutter context, it's "Paper, paper everywhere and not a place to think!" Stacks of newspapers, magazines, and assorted papers may not seem like clutter, but they are. If you don't believe me, just look around your home and office and take a mental inventory of all the stacks you have. Think of how much more floor, desk, and shelf space you'd have if they weren't there. When you're finally ready to get rid of those stacks of old newspapers and magazines, go through them one last time to make sure 1) you can live without it and 2) that your name, address, and any other personal information has been removed. Also remember to shred old bank statements or other documents that might give people access to your accounts. Nothing can hamper your lifestyle quicker than a case of identity theft.

For people who have an entrepreneurial spirit, garage sales and eBay are great outlets, and you have the benefit of connecting your "treasures" with people who will treasure them. In whatever way you choose to rid yourself of the extra weight of all this stuff, do it. The most important thing, for me, is that my clients get rid of some of the tangible things that are weighing them down. Too much accumulation tends to manifest itself in emotional weight. I'm not a psychologist, but I can tell you from personal experience that getting rid of dead weight has a way of making you feel lighter in body and spirit.

However, if you are a saver (I use the term "saver" intentionally instead of "hoarder," because that term suggests a very serious mental issue) and can't bear to part with a good deal of your stuff, it is still possible to de-clutter your home. That's why storage spaces were invented. But be bold about what you keep. Many people pay for a storage space for years and never have any use for what they put in there – another waste of money and mental energy!

Perspective is Key

Forging a fulfilling, sustainable lifestyle is difficult enough, but when you factor in a debilitating injury, it can seem nearly impossible to find that balance – except for my client, Ian. Ian was involved in a horrendous car accident when he was a teenager. It injured his spine, and it looked like he'd never walk again. However, after many surgeries and years of physical therapy, he has learned to walk again, though with a limp and a cane. Now he's in his early thirties, has graduated college, and lives on Long Island. After the accident, he received a large insurance payoff. This money, well invested, of course supports him, but he didn't allow himself to rest on his laurels. Ian, a very upbeat and energetic young man, had no intention of letting his injury, or the insurance money, keep him from living a full life.

While attending the University of South Carolina, Ian discovered that he had a knack for science. He first started tutoring his fellow students in nearly every scientific subject, from earth science to advanced physics, and eventually became a TA and completed an honor's thesis. Ian graduated among the top of his class, with many graduate schools vying for him. However, he didn't want a life in higher education – his passion was to teach high school students.

I was thrilled to work with and for a guy like Ian. In many ways he was my ideal client: energetic, passionate, and best of all willing to make the most out of his situation. The only bump in the road came when his parents got involved. One day Ian called me and said, "Paul, my father thinks my portfolio isn't doing too well. Can you check it out and see what the deal is?" I of course agreed. After all, it's my job to make sure portfolios are doing well. The odd thing was that I had recently checked Ian's portfolio and knew that it was fine, so I had a feeling that something else was churning under the surface.

Sometimes when clients call me up with reservations or worries about their portfolio, I get nervous. Did I miss something? Did something suddenly change without my knowledge? I pride myself on always being on top of every portfolio I handle, so if a client has a concern, I address it immediately. This one I took with a grain of salt. Whenever a client starts their sentence with, "My parents think..." there's a slight chance it's a case of worrywart syndrome. Even so, I went through Ian's portfolio again, and sure enough, it was as strong as ever. I checked his parents' portfolio too, since they were also my clients and theirs was doing great too.

A few months earlier, Ian referred me to his friend Chris, who Ian thought needed some help. Chris came to me with one plan in mind: he wanted to cash in all his stocks. I suggested we put in "stop losses," which he didn't want to do. He decided to pull out and have his assets sitting in cash. After some time I sent him a list of appropriate positions, all in the fixed income arena. He didn't respond.

Then Ian called me and said, "My friend Chris is in all cash and he's complaining that you're still charging him." I took a deep breath and tried to not get frustrated. I said, "Sometimes people pay me to not invest money. Maybe I would have been better off if I took Chris's money, put it into the market, allowed him to lose 40%, and then he'd be happy because he'd know he paid for a service."

Clearly exhausted by the whole scenario and hating to find himself put in the middle by his friend, Ian said, "I know how Chris can be." He might as well have said, "Don't shoot the messenger." I said, "All right, I'll call him." It was a long telephone call, but Chris and I worked everything out. Before I hung up, I made sure that he was very clear about what our arrangement was, moving forward.

Chris is a perfect example of someone with preconceived notions about how his portfolio was or should be performing, but really, it wasn't working well at all, until I came around. Once he let me do things the right way, we quickly made up for the income lost over the four months of "forced vacation" he put his money on!

Lifestyle in Later Life

Lifestyle refers to more than your monetary well being alone. And sometimes what you think is a financial conflict is actually rooted in more personal matters. These are issues and conflicts that can be just as troubling, if not more so, than mere finances. On that note, let me tell you the story of George.

To fully explain my relationship with George, I had been working with him for a while. He was a great client, and I got to know his entire family history, and managed his money, as well as the assets of his two sons. To be precise, I used to manage his sons' accounts too, but believe it or not, each of them died before their father: one from a skiing accident and the other from alcoholism. This poor guy, I thought. It is always devastating when a parent loses a child, but can you imagine losing both of your children in such tragic circumstances?

George lives half the time in Manhattan and the other half in Palm Springs. One day he called and said, "You've been great over the years, helping me out and offering me good advice. I want you to do more. Here's what I want to do. I want to give two charities a combined total of $6,000 a month. I want to set up a plan so that I can put money into these charities long after I'm gone." The two charities he was passionate about were the National Council on Alcohol and Drug Dependence and the Boys and Girls Club of America. It was amazing to me that a man who had gone through so much grief, and who clearly still carried around so much pain, could be so generous.

This was one of those rare times that a client came to me with a fully thought-out plan, and it actually sounded plausible. The problem was he was paying the charities currently using funds in his checking account. I told him, "Let's take whatever money you need, let's say a million, and put it into a Trust. I'll invest it for you, and instead of you using the principal and getting no rate of return on the money in your checking account, we can use it to build a portfolio. I believe I can create a distribution of around $6k a month in income from those investments for many years."

One of my more challenging situations involved a pair of brothers, Michael and Larry. They owned a couple of car dealerships, and they never got along – and neither did their wives. Their father was the one person that was able to keep them together, but once he died, the situation went from bad to worse. Their businesses suffered and finally the brothers decided that they needed to part ways. However, they were both extremely stubborn. They were working with the same CPA, and had agreed that one of the brothers had to buy the other out…but no one budged.

Finally, Michael came to me for help and explained the whole situation. He thought the CPA was favoring Larry, and he felt like he was being short-changed. I said I would set up a meeting with the CPA to hash this out. It was even worse than I thought – the CPA had told me that tensions between the brothers had gotten so high that they almost came to physical blows! We had a long meeting and hammered out a deal that both brothers would be happy with. Larry wound up buying out Michael's interest, and Michael was okay with that.

When tensions are high and it seems as if there is no possible solution, as was the case with Michael and Larry, it is crucial to involve an unbiased outside source, which is where the CPA and I came in. It was important that each brother felt represented in the matter. My ability to work with the CPA allowed us to create a fair deal so that everyone walked away happy.

Out With the Old, In With the New

Designing, implementing, and then maintaining a lifestyle that works for you can be difficult, especially during tumultuous times in your life. Whether your lifestyle change is prompted by an unexpected tragedy, a fortunate coincidence, or simply because you feel you're ready for it, it takes perseverance to enact this change and have it feel natural. A financial professional can help you get there and figure out the nuts and bolts, but it has to come first and foremost from within yourself. You can learn from your mistakes and from the mistakes my clients made, as presented in this book. Ultimately, it's about your knowing that you can live a happy, fulfilling life with more or less money, so long as you embrace change courageously, and always be fully appreciative of not only what money can buy, but also what it cannot buy.

"Be yourself, everyone else is already taken."

— Oscar Wilde

Afterword

Horizons: Get Ready to Find the Financial Advisor You Richly Deserve!

Congratulations! You've made your way through the book. I'll give you a moment to catch your breath, but make it quick because you still have quite a lot of work to do. Reading this book was a first, vital step in embarking on your financial journey, and now comes the hard part. However, with all of the advice, stories, and warnings I've shared with you, the "hard part" might actually seem easier!

I hope that my views on financial planning, retirement, and money matters in general have challenged you and shaken you loose from any preconceived notions you might have had. I commend you for taking an active interest in your financial future, and now that you've taken this big step, I hope you won't let all your newfound knowledge go to waste. It's time for you to use all of this fresh information and renewed enthusiasm for your money and your future and go out and start working towards your goals.

A Goal is a Goal, No Matter How Small

Many of the client stories I shared with you centered on retirement goals and planning, strengthening their portfolios, mobilizing their money to actually appreciate instead of stagnate, and taking measures to ensure their children are taken care of after they die. Some clients needed to adjust their views on insurance, while others needed to seriously re-evaluate their family dynamics. Of course, I've also shared my "worst case scenario" clients with you – the ones whose adult children may rely on them for longer than expected, or whose spending habits were sorely at odds with their financial reality. I shared stories about deeply mistrustful clients and of business partners who tried to undermine each other, even after decades of friendship, and while some of these stores might be unsettling, frustrating, or may have even struck a chord with you, I recounted each one for a specific purpose. I wanted to show you that no matter how dire your situation might seem, or even how perfect one's financial life might seem, more often than not, there's something hidden. This hidden element can completely uproot one's security – or perhaps it can be the missing link to fix one's problems. Either way, as a financial advisor, I insist on finding the root of the problem or the thing that's hidden and empowering you to take action.

As someone who has read this book, it is now your duty as a more financially informed person to look at your situation frankly and decide what you truly need to work on. Not only will having read this book give you a major advantage when you do have that first meeting with a financial professional, but I sincerely hope it will also give you the confidence to take some more risks moving forward.

Don't Wait – Act!

Perhaps you've found yourself in a less-than-advantageous situation and you need advice on how to mitigate it without causing even more damage. Maybe you're in the completely opposite scenario where you've recently come into a lot of money and don't know how to best invest, spend, or save it. Whatever your situation may be, don't wait for something dire to happen to start your financial journey. Many people put it off so long that it becomes difficult to correct the damage that has already been done.

I know it might be an intimidating process, but I hope that by reading this book, you now have the confidence to jump that first big hurdle.

Much like having an insurance policy, having a financial advisor on your side before an emergency occurs is always the best option. This way, in the event of a crisis – financial or otherwise – your advisor will be there. You'll always have someone on your side, operating with your best interests at heart. They will know your personal story inside and out, and will work with you to determine the best way to proceed and tackle any obstacles. Of course the idea is to limit some of those "emergencies" before they even arise! Financial emergencies, at least. Try as we might, we still can't fully predict or curb illnesses, accidents, or deaths. However, your financial professional can help you prepare for these events, in the unlikely event that they do occur.

I am not so naive that I will trust that everyone who reads this book will run out and book an appointment with a financial advisor immediately. I do hope, though, that this book has made you more aware of the pitfalls and bumps in the road that you can experience if you don't take the necessary measures to protect your assets.

Know Your History, Know Your Future

As you've read, one of the biggest life lessons I learned about money definitely came from my own family's experience. It was a fundamental moment for me, and a huge turning point where I realized that if my parents had done some planning it would have changed everything. All it takes is the awareness and impetus to change to propel you forward.

In that regard, I encourage you to mine your own family's financial history. Much like your physician will ask about your medical history to know what might be lurking beneath your skin and in your gene pool, it's extremely useful to examine how your family has dealt with money in the past. While not everyone is lucky enough to receive a lump sum inheritance, the ways in which you deal with money and overall spending habits might be inherited. Maybe you come from a long line of savers, in which case you might want to branch out and learn how to invest. But maybe you come from a long line of spenders, in which case you might want to explore retirement planning and other savings options.

It is always vital to stay true to yourself and your goals, but I encourage you to keep an open mind when it comes to financial advising. An advisor might offer suggestions that you are uncomfortable with, in which case you should speak up quickly. However, if his or her suggestions are different than what you are used to, but it truly seems like they are working to better your portfolio, proceed cautiously, ask plenty of questions, and take some risks if you feel so inclined. As Ralph Waldo Emerson once said, "Don't be too timid and squeamish about your actions. All life is an experiment. The more experiments you make the better."

Starting Off in the Right Direction

Here's a useful analogy for you. Let's say you're a movie producer and your goal is to produce an Oscar-winning film. You were able to cast Robert De Nero, Brad Pitt, Cate Blanchett and several other A-listers for the lead roles and you're working with a seemingly unlimited budget and a stellar script. However, when the movie gets released, it doesn't even come close to winning any awards, and is widely regarded as a flop. What went wrong? Well, you forgot about one of the most important aspects of the film – the director.

Not all financial advisors will actively "direct" you on how to use your money, but it is our job to be informed and to keep abreast of the financial climate. Advisors will know the best use of your portfolio at any given time, and will hopefully develop a trusting relationship with you. This way, their advice will encompass not only your portfolio's current status, but also your family's best interests. After all, it takes a special relationship to win that Oscar.

Remember the Basics

Vinny Lombardi, the legendary coach of the Green Bay Packers began more than one meeting saying, "Gentlemen, this is a football." I truly believe that starting from square one is the way to go. Before you write a symphony, you need to know how to play an instrument. Hey--you have to know what an instrument is!

Basically, what I'm saying here is that a lot of people want to start right off the bat with their big projects and investments, but don't know the first thing about the industry. This is how they wind up making huge mistakes and losing more than they would have if they had done some simple planning. You and your new advisor should be a well-oiled machine in terms of how you approach your portfolio. Of course there will be some growing pains, but after you get over that initial hump, you might be pleasantly surprised with how well it's going. And if it's not – if those growing pains never go away and instead get worse – maybe it's time to find a new advisor.

We already spoke at length about what "wealth" means to each person, but it's an important point that I hope I have driven home by now. It goes back to that "magic number" way of thinking. Again, it's not about the magic number – it's about how your amount is working for you. It is of course important to have goals, but you shouldn't let a number get in the way of your true goals.

I believe that people possess the power to make their own destinies in life, and that holds true for money as well. Of course I don't mean to say that everyone can be a billionaire if they simply try. No – what I mean is that everyone has the power to transform their financial reality, as long as they are willing to take some risks and put in some work. My hope is that this book has given you the confidence, knowledge, and most importantly the encouragement needed to take that big step. Don't wait for a "What If" to occur – start now!

By the way, I'm still in a band. I play the drums in a classic rock band, and we have never sounded better. This, for me, is the perfect way of blowing off steam from the intensity of my work. And keeping your money safe is intense!

"There came a time when the risk to remain tight in the bud was more painful than the risk it took to bloom."

— Anais Nin

About the Author

Paul S. Reback, founder and President of Capital Estate Advisors, Inc. has been enabling clients to achieve their financial goals and live their dreams for the past 30 years. Capital Estate Advisors, Inc. is a Registered Investment Advisory Firm (RIA) located in New York City. With all the right credentials—Paul is a Certified Financial Planner (CFP®)—he also brings a unique level of listening across the desk or on the phone, to each and every client interaction. With this kind of intense listening, he often hears what is not being said—by individual clients, partners, stockholders or between two halves of a couple with different agendas and risk tolerances. In addition to finding solutions to all financial challenges, helping people meet their goals and making sure they will never outlive their money, Paul is also notable for his willingness and ability to help clients in other areas of their lives with advice, counsel, and connection to other professionals in his extensive network, and any other resources.

Paul received his Certified Financial Planner designation from Adelphi University. He has been a guest lecturer at the American Institute of Certified Public Accountants and has taught continuing professional education courses for CPAs. A popular media expert, Paul has appeared on various radio and television talk shows, including Bloomberg Television, speaking on finance, investment, and estate and retirement planning. He has given many public talks and seminars to attorneys, physicians, stress management consultants and numerous other client advisors. He is a dynamic and entertaining speaker adept at making complex financial choices clearly understandable. Paul enjoys helping women entrepreneurs and professionals, and those women emerging after a divorce or the death of their spouse. He is adept at working with family owned businesses, and has written a white paper and prepared seminars for Dr. Steven Moyer's prestigious Network of Family Businesses, among others.

Paul believes the client should be informed and proactively involved in his/her financial affairs. To that end, he keeps the client continuously aware through ongoing client conversations and timely reviews. Of course, the best advice is not productive without action. After developing strategies based on your specific wants and needs Paul implements them, working through Fidelity Investments as his custodian.

For relaxation, Paul, an accomplished drummer, performs with his classic rock group, "Paul's Power," at various clubs and other venues. As another way to give back, Paul serves as a Trustee with the Free and Accepted Masons of the State of New York. He has served as a board member with Samaritan Foundation, a non-profit organization that supports community-based substance abuse services, including special services for the homeless, veterans, women and the mentally challenged. He designed, runs and performs at a fundraiser for the benefit of the Fire Dept. of New York (FDNY), every year on September 11th. Paul is also a trustee and board member of The Bronx Museum of the Arts.

Paul is the proud father of Catherine Reback, a recent graduate of Miami University, Oxford, Ohio.

"I've learned that people will forget what you said, people will forget what you did, but people will never forget how you made them feel."

— *Maya Angelou*

About Capital Estate Advisors

Specializing in Asset Management & Wealth Preservation.

Founded in 1993 by Paul S. Reback, Capital Estate Advisors, Inc., located in New York City, is an independent Registered Investment Advisory (RIA) firm with securities transactions handled through our custodian, Fidelity Investments. We provide expertise in asset management, estate planning and wealth preservation and growth.

Paul and his team proudly believe that the key to the firm's success with a wide spectrum of clients is evidenced by their long-term relationships with clients and their clients' enthusiastic referrals of family, friends and associates—people who likewise wish to both grow and protect their assets while maintaining their preferred lifestyles. The firm's uniquely personal approach begins by listening carefully to your needs and goals. The CEA team becomes deeply engaged and involved, helping each client identify and realize his/her intentions in both the near and long-term.

This is a very personal business, and continued financial success and peace of mind begins with a strategy specific to you. Clients may be experiencing a major life transition, selling a business or buying property, anticipating retirement, intent on helping their adult children or sending their grandchildren to college, eager to take more time to travel or otherwise enjoy life—and want to make sure their money will always be there to support their intentions and dreams.

The company is a fee-based advisory firm with no hidden

agendas on what to sell you and no cookie-cutter, one-size-fits-all advice. They are proud of their long-standing membership in Fidelity Investments, through which they enact any stock and bond transactions to be made on your behalf.

Capital Estate Advisors will also consult and coordinate activities with attorneys, accountants, trust officers, pension and 401(k) specialists and investment bankers, as necessary and appropriate. Paul will work with your other advisors to navigate the complexities of estate planning, charitable giving and generation skipping techniques through the proper use of trusts and estate liquidity funding techniques.

As Paul explains, "Our role is to manage your assets in a way that is always specific to you. Our primary motivation is the right balance of capital growth and preservation—objectives that are not mutually exclusive."

Come in for a free consultation and discover the CEA difference!

For more information visit www.paulreback.com.

NOTES: